Should Anyone
Say Forever?

Should Anyone Say Forever?

On Making, Keeping and Breaking Commitments

John C. Haughey, S.J.

Doubleday & Company, Inc.
Garden City, New York
1975

Library of Congress Cataloging in Publication Data

Haughey, John C
Should anyone say forever?

1. Commitment (Psychology)   I. Title.
BF619.H37   241'.6'7
ISBN 0-385-09754-9
Library of Congress Catalog Card Number 74–12690

Contents

Contents

Introduction

The purpose of this study will be to isolate the factor of commitment in human lives in order to examine its value. We will attempt to discover something of the nature of interpersonal commitments, as well as some of the factors that go into making, keeping or breaking them.

But human commitment is too unwieldy a subject to deal with. Virtually every expression of intention is called a commitment today. Since the word is overused, we must narrow it down to indicate the area of our concentration. Our interest here will be only with interpersonal commitments—those that people make to one another. But I mean to be even more specific and not include any and every commitment people make to people. We will not deal, for example, with the enormously important area of the social commitment we owe to those who are poor or in need of our service. We will, moreover, concentrate our attention only on those interpersonal commitments that people take to be primary in their lives. These will usually be to a spouse, or a friend, or in some cases to a community, or to God. Or a combination of these. Ordinarily a person's commitment to God will be a special kind of interpersonal commitment, as we will have occasion to show in the course of this study. We are not dealing here with impersonal commitments—those made in abstraction from people—such as a commitment to an ideology or a career or a task or an organization or to some ideal or value.

People will approach this study with wildly different expectations and needs. There are those who are sure that the notion of commitment is as obsolete as the covered wagon and will look for a study of this kind to say that. They will be disappointed, surely, because I do not think this is so. There are others who have been ever ready to make a commitment of themselves but wonder why they have never been able to get it together with anyone. Such a reader will find that this treatment of commitment will not get into the kind of "how-to" particulars such a person is seeking. One who feels he needs a clear statement to justify his disengagement from a commitment he has made will probably be looking for more support than he will find here. And those who feel that society has already gone too far and its citizenry has grown too fickle about their commitments will be disconcerted when they find the stern, strict approach of yesteryear missing from these pages.

The person who finds himself troubled about the subject, for whatever reasons, will find here things to ponder which perhaps he would not have thought of before. This study could prove helpful for those who resist committing themselves at all by enabling them to see something other than negative factors in the committed life. In addition to balkers, it might also encourage the undercommitted to face up to their neglect and the overcommitted to recognize their malady. And if it helps to sort out the issues for some who are uncertain about the merits of the commitments they have already made, the study will be worthwhile. In general, these reflections are meant to be in dialogue with the ponderings that go on deep within a person who, for whatever reasons, has begun to wonder about commitments—his own or others'.

Let the reader reflect on the elusiveness of the subject for a moment. It would seem, for example, that on the face of it, keeping one's commitments is more honorable than breaking them. How explain, then, the fact that so often we have made heroes out of those who have broken their commitments? Saul of Tarsus did, as did Daniel Ellsberg and the Duke of Windsor and Martin Luther and the pilots who refused to accept missions over Cambodia and Laos. They all reneged on commitments. They did so, of course, in the name of some higher commitment. Is commitment, therefore, a wholly subjective thing? Is fidelity or infidelity in the eye of the beholder only? An interview with Henry the Eighth on the subject of St. Thomas More would lead one to believe that it was.

On the other hand, we find the failure to keep one's commitments reprehensible, even loathsome at times. The laws of our society reflect this as the preponderant judgment. The whole fabric of social existence is being shredded by the failure of people to keep their word. A society in which vows are abandoned, promises broken, oaths disregarded and contracts violated cannot long endure. Perseverance in commitment is the cohesive force that

9

keeps social interaction from falling into chaos. At the same time, have you ever considered the countless lives that are ruined by those who follow through with commitments they have once made though their hearts are no longer in them? While seeming virtuous to the rest of society, the cruelest form of behavior can at times be perseverance.

A further perplexing aspect of this elusive subject is that the less conscious one is of his or her commitment the more likely one is to be content with it. Concentration on one's commitment can be a sign of tension, an indication that the commitment is in jeopardy or that motivation for persevering in it is beginning to fade. It is quite likely, therefore, that the wrong way to attack problems of commitment is to address oneself to it as a subject. When someone is wondering about the *whether* or *what* or *when* of it, it could be a sign that it is either too soon to take the plunge or too late to keep the commitment that was once made. By concentrating on the commitment aspect of a relationship there is a better-than-even chance that what was begun in love will be continued out of a sense of obligation, if continued at all. In many ways the words of a sage about another subject apply here: "I would rather feel compunction than have to define it." I would rather be committed than have to figure out the nature of it. For once the spontaneity, the connaturality has gone out of it, the person all too often continues committed to his commitment rather than to the person he initially gave his word to.

In the initial stages of the preparation of this manuscript I was bothered by a nagging doubt about the universality of the question. I wondered: Is this only a problem with the middle generation and therefore one that dates the inquirer? Would members of the younger generation consider it passé, something redolent of the Victorian Era? And do not most of those older than the middle generation wonder why it is a question at all, since it seems that in their day commitment was a black-and-white issue for the majority? But such doubts always gave way to the ever-recurring conviction that commitment is as thoroughly and endemically a human question as health or mortality or love or security. For even those young people who are keenest to be free of commitments rely on the commitments of others. Those who feel free to disparage the notion of commitment, if they reflect on it, have grown tall on the strengths of others. They rely on others remaining steady while they exercise their right to remain free of everyone. It seems to me that we are all like gymnasts in a human pyramid. We all expect the fragile human base immediately below us to remain stable so that we can crawl a level higher without the lower tier collapsing. What the young see and rightly rail against is that in previous generations so much that passed for commitment was really the product of conditioning or manipulation or ignorance or fear. But in their attempt to transcend these unhappy conditions which often had people live in a less than human way, too many now seem prepared to dismiss without examination the significance of commitment in human life. In other words, I did not long entertain the doubts I had about the universal relevance of the subject.

This is an intriguing subject, for everyone is involved somehow or other in the reality of it. There isn't anyone who is not committed to something or someone. Even

those who are adamant about the need to stay free of
commitments have to commit themselves to following
their own particular notions of what will leave them free
and uncommitted. The phenomenon is as broad as it is
long, including all who are living and all who ever lived,
although many would not be conscious of doing so under
the particular rubric of commitment.

Even clearer than its universality is the uniqueness of
each person's commitments. Reflect for a moment on the
immense variety of objects people commit themselves to,
the disparity of their motivations in keeping them, or the
complexity of the intentions that had them make the commitments they made in the first place. And do any two
people mean the same thing when they give their word or
profess their intentions, even when their vow formulas are
identical? In fact, commitments are unique and so completely individual that one wonders whether anything
could be said about the subject that abstracts from the individual and applies to the many. I believe it can and that
a greater degree of intelligibility is needed in this whole
area than we presently have access to. Nevertheless,
throughout this study I hope to remain sensitive to the ultimate uniqueness and inviolability of each person's commitments.

The reader should be warned at the outset that the subject will not receive an *objective* treatment. Neither the
writer nor the reader can stand completely apart from the
subject and inspect it as if it were an object susceptible of
clinical inquiry. Both writer and reader are part of the
data. We are immersed in it, as it were, benefiting and
suffering from it. We are the beneficiaries and victims of
the entire web of commitments that have been honored

and broken by others and ourselves. What I claim to see, therefore, will be colored by the history of my own commitments, my fidelity, and my failures in this regard as well as the fidelity and infidelity of those who have touched my life. And the reader's own commitment history will be operating in the way he or she responds to the pages that follow. The reader would be well advised, therefore, to approach the subject more as a contemplative who expects to glimpse something of a mystery of which he is a part than as a spectator viewing a phenomenon over against himself.

At this point I would like to make my first positive affirmation about the nature of interpersonal commitment. It is at the core of the mystery that every person is. The subject matter of our study, therefore, must be affirmed as part of the mystery of the person that cannot or should not be disgorged from that center. It can be contemplated but not penetrated. One must approach a person's commitment with the same reverence each human being deserves. We associate mystery, perhaps, with our ignorance and insufficiency. But that association is unfortunate and inaccurate. We are not a mystery because of any insufficiency in ourselves—of insight or intellect or whatever. We are a mystery because we are not confined to the here and now. We are not limited by what we are now or know now. Illimitability is written into every aspect of our living.

The comprehensible, or the comprehended, on the other hand, is by definition limited. It is capable of being mastered, defined, penetrated. But each new moment of comprehension only creates newer questions and enlarges the area of the mystery of the person. If at the end of this study, therefore, the reader has a new degree of understanding about interpersonal commitment, and at the same time allows it to remain a mystery that is radically impenetrable, then the study will be successful, as far as I am concerned.

A final introductory note. The subject of commitment is the province of no single academic discipline. Certainly we have something to learn about it from sociology and history, anthropology and ethics, philosophy and psychology. The reflections in this study have benefited from writings in all of these fields. I have found Christian theology more helpful than any of the other disciplines, however, perhaps because I am a theologian. Nevertheless, I do not present these reflections to the reader in the dress of scientifically-arrived-at theology. While the texture of the thought in this work will be for the most part theological, the line of argument is not developed for theologians as such. It is meant rather for people who have reason to ponder the subject matter and who wish to take theological reflections into account in their ponderings.

Should Anyone
Say Forever?

Chapter I
The Underpinnings

Some observations on the vast subject of human relationships seem to be the best place to begin a study on commitment since it is from our relationships to one another that our commitments arise. From there we will look at the act of commitment itself by examining the underpinnings and structure of such an act.

As a people we Americans are famous the world over for our ability to enter into spontaneous relationships with others. If I might be allowed to generalize, it seems that we make acquaintances rapidly and enjoy a ready capacity for personal exchange and are eager, by and large, to disregard the barriers of formality. But the next step, let us call it generically friendship, we take less well. Americans who have lived in Europe for any length of time, for example, are usually struck with the relatively greater interest in friendship the average European seems to have than the average American. Friendship seems more important to most Europeans, so it is cultivated more intently, and more time and energy are devoted to it because obviously a higher priority is put on it. If this observation is accurate, it seems to me that our overdeveloped facility for acquaintanceship and our underdeveloped capacity for companionship and friendship adds to many of America's social ills. For a commitment to another person will only be as successful and as rewarding as the relationship from which it arises. And if we are living in a culture in which relationships all too frequently remain superficial, then we should not expect miracles when the formality of commitment is brought to such relationships. But this is the kind of transformation many seem to expect from commitments.

The best atmosphere and the ideal preparation for interpersonal commitment is, I believe, the development of depth in, and capacity for, companionship and friendship. If we were more versed in this art, we would be more perceptive about the commitments we make and, therefore, more successful in keeping our commitments to one another. I wonder how many of the 980,000 American marriages that ended in divorce last year began in such an atmosphere and with the requisite depth? When these are wanting, misperceptions abound. Mutual desire, for example, is read as the mutuality of love, and commitments made on that ill-conceived basis are not long sustained.

There are numerous indications that the contemporary mores of relationships are leading to dissatisfaction on a wide scale, dangerously wide for the stability of our culture. The widespread interest in the "open marriage" concept is one of these indicators. This desire to pursue some degree of intimacy outside of marriage in more than one relationship is inevitable when so many marriages come about before the socialization process of companionship and friendship has seasoned the parties to make a wise choice of a marriage partner. The irony is that the marriage commitment can block subsequent social maturation if the partners look solely to each other to have their needs met, and outside friendships are seen as incompatible with their marriage relationship.

Marriage is not the only place where this dissatisfaction is showing up. Life in the convent has been too impoverishing, precisely in the area of relationships, for 30,000 Roman Catholic women religious in this country in the last ten years. So dissatisfying, in fact, that they withdrew from their commitments and departed religious life. Loneliness, lack of support from other sisters, and the need for intimacy were among the most frequently cited reasons for this departure (according to a recent study conducted by the National Sisters' Vocation Conference).

In brief, then, if we are concerned about questions of commitment, we must be equally attentive to the quality of relationships from which these commitments arise and within which they are lived-out.

Bear in mind that we are dealing in this study with more than just the interpersonal commitments made in marriage. These others tend to be less determinate than marriage, but they are commitments nonetheless. There is quite a difference between a companionship or friendship in which there is a commitment to one another and one in which there is not. Without a commitment the relationship relies completely on spontaneity, mutual interests, and the convenience of circumstances whereas a companionship or a friendship in which there is a commitment can withstand distances and long periods of absence. It determines circumstances rather than being determined by them. A commitment begins to be shaped as a spontaneous relationship becomes more fully chosen and more consciously cultivated. It develops from its initial stages into a fully constituted "we." Whether the commitment is marital in form or more akin to the category of friendship, it involves a specification of one's life to a greater or lesser extent.

But such a specification must be examined. Is such a narrowing down of one's potential choices necessary? Does commitment enhance the possibilities of growth or does it inhibit them? The answer, of course, depends on the one committing himself and those to whom he is committed. But, abstracting from individuals, I believe several observations can be made immediately. Withholding oneself from committing oneself has not proven beneficial to those swinging singles studied by George Gilder in his recent work *Naked Nomads* (Quadrangle, 1974). He concludes that "the failure of the singles ideal is a major sociological fact of the last decade." Rather graphically, the Gilder study marshals overwhelming statistics to prove that "depression, addiction, disease, disability, psychiatric treatment, loneliness, insomnia, institutionalization, poverty, discrimination, unemployment and nightmares . . . are the dirty sheets and unmade mornings" of the majority of swinging single males in the United States.

In reading Gilder's book I could not help but be reminded of the Gospel observation ". . . the road that leads to perdition is wide and spacious, and many take it" (Matt. 7:13). This and the Gilder findings suggest that noncommitment is destructive of the individual, that meandering is a refusal of life. By contrast, Jesus exhorts his listeners to "enter by the narrow gate" since this alone "leads to life" (Matt. 7:13–14). The narrow gate Jesus was alluding to probably refers to the gate in Jerusalem which could only accommodate people unaccompanied by their possessions and camels and donkeys. It was so small that it was a "people only" passageway. The metaphor suggests that life will be found when a person is willing to particularize his choices in life and does so in such a way that he does not identify himself in terms of what he has or hopes to hold on to but in terms of who he is and who he intends to be present to. He chooses to enter the kingdom of persons and does so through particular people.

I say the passage suggests this line of reasoning, but it is perhaps too secular an interpretation of what Jesus said. One needs further evidence to establish the positive value of interpersonal commitment. In what follows we shall attempt to compile some of this by analyzing the act of commitment in order to see more clearly what it is and whether it is something to be made or avoided.

There are some aspects about a commitment that are incontrovertible. First of all it is obvious that every commitment involves a choice. Our commitments are our most formal choices. If we can see the role choices play in self-development and the role of nonchoice in personal underdevelopment, we can begin to see the significance of commitments since they are our choices writ large. In the same way, and for the same reason, we will examine the nature of a promise since every commitment also involves a promise. Finally, we will address ourselves to the problem of reconciling freedom with commitment.

21

EVERY COMMITMENT IS A CHOICE

The role that a choice plays in the life of a person, for a moment and briefly, the commitment plays over a longer period of time. Our choices, more than any other act or operation of our faculties individuate and define us. To borrow our imagery from the book of Genesis, we might say that just as the Spirit hovered over the formless void in the beginning of the universe, so also in the beginning of the individual's own history his spirit can be imagined as hovering over the formless void of the self. Just as each determination of the Spirit gave the universe its shape, so also by each act of personal choice the spirit of the individual begins to form the void of the self, ordering the chaos and shaping his person. Notwithstanding all appearances to the contrary, an individual does not become a person by growing upward physically, outward spacially, or inward reflectively. Selfhood comes to be primarily by choosing. By failing to choose, by remaining in a constant state of indecision, a person's spirit is vaporous and, as it were, apart from him, hovering.

In the act of choosing, most of all, the spirit of a person stands forth and is enfleshed. Our choices express our self-understanding and at the same time make self-understanding possible. By contrast, nonchoosers and half choosers are a puzzle to themselves and to others. Their spirit has not yet assumed its rightful place. They live in the immature condition of wanting to "play everything by ear." They dance when another pipes, and wail when another determines that a dirge is called for. An individual who is insufficiently self-determining will find that his milieu, his family, his appetites, or any other force external to himself, usurp the place and function his own spirit should assume.

All of this is easy to see in the early years of a person's life when his future and selfhood are still so amorphous. But it never ceases to be true throughout a person's life. Any time choice is called for and turned away from, the chaos of indefiniteness can reappear and one's spirit can again become a hoverer.

Men have battled for centuries against slavery in the firm belief that its involuntary form of determinism is evil. The irony of our present age is that so many people, though free to do otherwise, allow themselves to become afflicted with the voluntary slavery of indetermination.

The Church has been consistently adamant about the evil of wrong choices. And in her preachments about sin the Church has taught the imminence of hell's fire for those who have made wrong choices and committed themselves to objects that were immoral. But she has not given equal attention to what seems to be a much greater flaw in the contemporary character—that is, nonchoice, indecision, noncommitment. Perhaps she can be exonerated on the grounds that the people she ministered to in previous generations were not quite so prone to live their lives as nonchoosers and tentative choosers, as our own age seems to be increasingly.

When the refusal to choose leaves the work of God's hands unfinished, then this peculiar kind of inaction takes on a moral dimension. Why? Because the unique way of manifesting some aspect of the fullness of God that every person is born to manifest remains mere potency. Refusal to come to the point of decision, choice, or commitment can leave something of creation itself unfinished and hence God's glory incomplete. This constitutes evil at the level of being itself. An individual thwarts the purpose of God's creating him by refusing to exercise the cocreatorship that he could exercise. That which is called forth by God is being rendered void by man. Martin Buber has written eloquently about the evil of indecision.[1] Buber would say that reality at any one moment is capable of becoming unreality if the person allows the chaos of "possibilities" to envelop him, imposing its "form of indefiniteness upon the definiteness of the moment." In his own picturesque way, Buber claims that it is through decision that "the soul as form" overcomes the "soul as matter." Through decision, "chaos is subdued and shaped into cosmos."

Why does this malady of indecision have such a strong hold on so many moderns? Whence this new widespread affliction of indeterminacy? There are many factors and reasons. One of the main reasons for the incapacity or cynicism about personal decision-making for many Americans can be traced to their years of schooling. The extension of the years of education is an extension of the years of dependency, and extended dependency institutionalizes indecision. Even after the ever-lengthening years of schooling are over, the occupational and vocational choices of the people, insofar as there are any, are contingent upon the treacherously vagrant economic conditions of society.

The growing size, complexity, and impersonality of social institutions—whether people find it in their work, in their dealings with civic agencies, or all too frequently in

[1] Martin Buber, *Good and Evil* (New York: Charles Scribner's Sons, 1953), esp. pp. 99–139.

their churches—tend to create a sense of futility in many individuals about their capacity to determine their own lives. What value has personal intention or purpose or aim or decision when it continually runs up against a Big Brother institution which, it seems, is continually narrowing down the area of freedom or trying to determine virtually every aspect of one's life? One can wonder why one should invest anything of oneself in major choices when one sees the lives of so many people engineered, conditioned, determined, and thwarted by institutional decisions. When one comes to feel that ultimately what one decides won't count for much, one is not likely to assign much importance to deciding anything.

A number of historical factors have also helped to introduce a softness into contemporary society about the power of personal choice. We have come a long way since the Victorian Era when people believed (or at least spoke as if they believed) that "where there's a will there's a way." The pristine reputation that will power once enjoyed was only gradually destroyed. Two of its main defamers were Charles Darwin and Sigmund Freud. Darwin's discoveries about man's evolution gave rise to the physical sciences, especially biology and chemistry, which within one century have dramatically changed man's view of himself. Once human existence is seen as intricately interwoven with, and of a piece with, the rest of the material universe, then the force that will power was supposed to exert on matter is seen in a new light: much less powerful, more determined than determining.

Freud's discovery of the unconscious was even more damaging than Darwin's discovery of evolution. Freud saw how much of what men had hitherto ascribed to freedom and will power was in actuality being influenced by something oozing up from below, something he called the unconscious. He claimed that this influence shaped the life of a person in ways never before suspected. "The deeply rooted belief in psychic freedom and choice," Freud observed, "is quite unscientific and must give ground before the claims of a determinism which governs mental life."[2] Freud set out to show that what Victorians had ascribed to will power was really traceable to drives and desires the basis of which the human agent was unaware. Seeing how often will power was used in the service of repression, Freud developed psychoanalysis as an anti-will system, as Rollo May has observed.[3] Silvan Tomkins of Princeton University has remarked in the same vein: "Psychoanalysis is a systematic training in indecision."[4]

So much for the place of choice and the effect and causes of indecision on the individuation of the person. Because every commitment is at the very least a choice, these observations should serve as initial indicators of the importance of commitments in life.

EVERY COMMITMENT IS A PROMISE

There is no need to search out the historical or psychological or sociological reasons why people are reluctant to make promises. The projection of oneself into the future

[2] Sigmund Freud, General Introduction to Psychoanalysis (New York: Garden City Publishing Co., 1938), p. 95.
[3] Rollo May, Love and Will (New York: W. W. Norton & Co., Inc., 1969), p. 182. "The inherited basis of our capacity for will and decision has been irrevocably destroyed. And, ironically . . . when power has grown so tremendously and decisions are so necessary and so fateful . . . we find ourselves lacking any new basis for will."
[4] Ibid., p. 194.

by making promises is an action that has been reluctantly undertaken since time began. It has always been bewitchingly easy to believe that one's freedom is preserved by tying as few knots as possible, and that perfect freedom means tying no knots at all.

The simple act of promising has something to teach us about commitment. The promise is a particular kind of choice. Unlike every other choice we make, what is unique about a promise is that it describes something we intend to do in the future, whereas any other choice is a formal determination about the present. By a promise one projects oneself into the future. Every commitment involves a promise. The most formal promises we make are commitments. The one making a promise is expressing his faith in his own power to do what he wills to do. He is saying that his will is capable of remaining constant with regard to what he has promised and that he will find within himself the wherewithal to do what he said he would do when the time comes to do it. The one making a promise is not understood to be making a prediction about himself, he is asserting his firm intention. He is not merely describing his present state of mind but is binding himself to a future course.

Every promise, therefore, binds the one who makes it to some future action. By giving his word he is assuming an obligation, but he does more than that. He yields to another, or others, a claim over himself by creating an expectation in them concerning what he says he will do for (or to or with) them.[5] Therefore, the person promising constitutes something in the order of being itself, some-

[5] Sister Margaret A. Farley, "A Study in the Ethics of Commitment Within the Context of Theories of Human Love and Temporality" (Doctoral Dissertation, Yale University, 1974), esp. pp. 50–89.

thing between himself and another or himself and the group to whom the promise is communicated. A new relationship or network of relationships, consequently, is thus created.

It would be superficial to let an analysis of the promise rest merely in terms of the obligations that promises entail. By making promises, a person goes far beyond the obligatory and beyond the here and now. He is saying to those to whom he gives his word that he is in charge of his own life and that he freely chooses to use his freedom to project himself into the future in the specific manner which he determines. He gives his word because he is free to do so and does so freely. But the word he gives puts him in communion with others. His word given takes on flesh. His future and the future of others are now intertwined by his own determination and intention.

Rather than see this in a negative light, we should realize that the capacity of human beings to make and keep promises is also the surest way they have to free themselves, to determine themselves rather than be determined. To hold that one should not project oneself into the future by promise suggests that a person must be imprisoned in the present. One puts oneself and others at the mercy and whim of the moment. By withholding one's word one withholds one's self. One becomes a bystander in the drama of human existence, or a participant on a merely provisional basis. Even if one does not subscribe to these statements theoretically, in practice one shows agreement with them by refusing to project oneself into the future by making promises. One is equivalently prizing isolation over communion then, and preserving oneself rather than giving oneself. All of one's treasure then must come from the present rather than the future.

What people mean when they say "I promise" determines the quality of social existence. Society is as fragile or as durable as the meaning people assign to promise-words. Furthermore, the same words on the lips of different people can have considerably different connotations. They can weave a heinously intricate web of opportunism or a finely spun social fabric. At one time there was a clear enough meaning to the promise-words people used. Not that they always kept their word, but when they broke it there was no denying it by them or by others.

In her book *The Human Condition,* Hannah Arendt pinpoints the two factors that she finds essential to preserving life from chaos. The first deals with the past: Forgiveness is needed for the undoing of mistakes of the past. The second concerns the future: the faculty of making and keeping promises. Her concern is with the effect upon the social order if promises come to mean anything less than what tradition has understood them to mean. The making and keeping of promises are an expression of one of the most ancient needs of man, according to this philosopher. In fact, the two great institutions of Western society were built on promises. The Judeo-Christian religion grew out of the covenant promise God made to Abraham. And the Roman Empire built a legal system based on the inviolability of agreements and treaties. Human beings, both to ensure their own survival and to make their societies increasingly hospitable, have gone out from themselves to their fellows in promise and covenant since these times and long before. People have come to rely on and to count on the communion created by the words they give to one another. Promise is what holds society together and staves off barbarity, according to Miss Arendt.

In brief, one dimension of every commitment is that it is a promise. As promises, our commitments project us into the future. They also create a communion between ourselves and those to whom we have given our word. Our promises and commitments free us from being wholly locked into the present. Finally, we looked briefly at the social ramifications of making and keeping promises.

FREEDOM AND COMMITMENT

Although the foregoing are essential areas to reflect on, we have still not gotten to the heart of the problem of commitment by our analysis of either a choice or a promise. For there are many who choose continually, who are decisive, but who refuse to make the kind of choice that a commitment is. And there are many who are willing to make promises and who promise frequently, but who keep their promises according to a gauge that is novel, if the norms of fidelity we have inherited from the past are any indication of what fidelity is. A third factor, therefore, must be examined to complete our preliminary analysis of the act of commitment. Both refusal to make commitments and unfaithfulness in keeping commitments that have been made are usually the consequence of the notion of freedom the person entertains. Therefore, the need to examine contemporary notions of freedom.

On the face of it, it would seem that freedom and commitment are incompatible, or so the wisdom concocted by our age would have us believe. As with so many other values in our culture, it is difficult to capture the notions behind the prevailing mood about freedom. But several of the axioms about freedom that seem to be embraced by many of our contemporaries would be expressed in ways such as these: 1) If one would preserve one's freedom, let him fight shy of committing himself. 2) The greater the number of options a person has, the greater the freedom he enjoys. 3) All a person must do to increase his freedom is to augment his capacity for having his own way. 4) Freedom is the capacity for indefinite revision, the ability to be always doing something different. 5) Since freedom and commitment are incompatible in this life, we must settle for one or the other.

In order to deal with these contemporary attitudes about freedom, it might be helpful to distinguish the different ways in which freedom is talked about. Freedom can refer to the individual's capacity to be self-determining. Or the word can refer to the feeling of freedom one has because of the context he is in, i.e., he finds himself in a set of circumstances in which a number of options are open to him. And thirdly, freedom can refer to the act of choice itself: the experience of freely choosing this or that object.

With regard to the first category, the capacity for self-determination, several things should be said. First of all, a person who imagines himself to enjoy a freedom that is never specified believes in a freedom that eventually cannot exist. Human freedom is not some phantom commodity that enjoys a life apart from particulars. Freedom must be exercised in order to be. "Freedom is not the capacity for indefinite revision for always doing something different," Karl Rahner has observed, "but the capacity that creates something final, something irrevocable and eternal."[6] Secondly, once one's capacity for self-determination is exercised, the object chosen will in turn determine the person. We are free to choose, but we are not free to reconstitute the reality of the object chosen by us. It will stamp us with its shape. The objects of our choices specify us. Or, as the saying goes: We become what we love. Thirdly, our capacity to be self-determining creatures has a social history which antedates all of us. But this history acts as a deterrent to the proper exercise of freedom. Our capacity to be self-determining does not come down to us in a pristine state. We have inherited the misuse of freedom known classically as original sin. This wound limits our capacity for self-determination and has the effect of both blurring our perceptions of what is good for us and weakening our desire to choose the good.

There are also limitations in the second meaning of freedom noted above, the one which refers to freedom in a context. The point to be made here is that no one's freedom exists apart from a particular context. Furthermore, there is no such thing as finding oneself in a context in which an infinite number of possibilities are open to one. Just as freedom in the first sense must get down to particulars, freedom in this second sense must always face the particulars one's life is circumscribed by. Every context is circumscribed logistically, geographically, historically, and socially, to mention only a few of the factors limiting it. Each person's attempt to be a self-determining individual does not take place within a vacuum but within an increasingly complex and dense set of circumstances. Every individual's exercise of freedom changes

[6] Karl Rahner, *Grace in Freedom* (New York: Herder and Herder, 1969), p. 80.

the shape of his neighbor's freedom, and vice versa. It might enlarge it or constrict it; the point here is merely that it affects it.

And, finally, a comment on the third meaning of freedom—the property of freedom in the acts one undertakes. It is only in the exercise of one's freedom that one assures it; by nonexercise one runs the risk of losing it. To attempt to live one's life in a state of indetermination is the surest way of becoming unfree, because then one will be determined by forces outside oneself. Our freedom, once exercised, furthermore, always becomes part of the history that is ourselves. To ask for any other configuration of myself to reality would be tantamount to asking that my word not be listened to, that my actions be disregarded, or that my person be taken without seriousness. Since we would not have others regard our freedom or our person so cavalierly, neither should we take our own freedom so disparagingly.

The purpose of these comments has not been to make distinctions that might appear merely academic, but to demythologize the meaning of freedom. If it is not rooted in the realities of social, historical, and personal existence, freedom begins to take on an allure and an unreality that make its attainment impossible.

We can now return to the axioms about freedom with which this section began and begin to question their validity. Where better to place them than at the bar of our own experience? Are uncommitted people freer people, in fact? Does one who insists on keeping all his or her options open enjoy the depth of relationship he seeks? Does he not find himself, rather, linked with others equally unwilling to surrender their autonomy? What depths can a relationship reach if one cannot fully convince another that he is not "in it" for himself? Only a fool would give much of himself or herself to an opportunist.

A number of the axioms about freedom are generated by the sexual emancipation we are going through in modern times. There is a growing body of evidence that our enlightenment about sex is not very enlightened and that our newly won freedom is creating much misery. Even the most tantalizing aspect of the emancipation vision—that of the unfettered, "swinging" singles—is coming in for a re-examination as we have noted earlier.

But if their opposite numbers, the marrieds, are so happy, how explain the 980,000 divorces in the United States last year? Does not experience reveal to us that there are innumerable people who, though in a situation that looks like one of commitment, are unfree? A little closer examination would indicate, I think, that it is difficult to establish a causal relationship between their commitments and their unfreedom. Certainly, if one or both parties are simulating commitment to one another or withholding themselves from really committing themselves to one another, then the commitment cannot be considered the source of the problem since it isn't being made in effect. Undercommitment is leaving one or both partners unhappy and unfree.

There are obviously as many reasons for divorce as there are divorces, but the only question we have to deal with here is whether marital discontent can be traced to incompatibility between freedom and commitment. I do not believe it can, but uncovering the actual causes would require a case-by-case study. Suffice it to say here that the problems in marriage are always traceable to the individual spouses or to the relationship between them. As regards the first of these two alternatives, it should be obvious that if the individual is an unfree person, he or she will not create a free and freeing situation in marriage. By the same token, the marriage will be only as free as the individuals contracting it. Moral and psychological deficiencies, such as infidelity and jealousy and feelings of insecurity, strain the bond between spouses sometimes to the breaking point. More often than not, those to whom an unfree person has linked himself are made to feel the onus for the individual's deficiency as a self-determining person. The commitment between them can become a convenient whipping boy. It can be made to bear the blame when something in the individual is missing.

The problem can also be traceable to the relationship itself. If it was too immature as a relationship in the ways described at the beginning of the chapter, certainly it is presumptuous to ask it to sustain a commitment. Some commitments were unwise from the start because of a lack of compatibility between the partners and no amount of attention can turn them into occasions of happiness for either. There are also marriages in which the partners are expecting too much of one another. This can lead to the unfreeing situation of overcommitment which will be discussed in the next chapter.

In brief, none of the above instances argues that freedom and commitment are incompatible. On the contrary, it can be seen that unfreedom and commitment are incompatible as also are freedom and noncommitment. As Rahner observed, our freedom exists in order to create something, something "irrevocable and eternal." The same paradox stalks the person who seeks to preserve his freedom by not using it as confronts the man who seeks to save his life by not giving himself to life. One who would be free must sooner or later face the issue of the narrow gate.

Chapter II
Components of Commitment

We are still in the foothills of the subject of commitment. A commitment, at least as it is specified in this study, is much more than a choice. It is also considerably more complex than a simple promise. And in many instances it is difficult to see how it is a source of freedom. Unless, therefore, we take these reflections further and deeper, we will have failed to do justice to the subject matter of this study.

THE PRIMORDIAL LEVEL OF COMMITMENT

Having become interested in this subject a few years ago, I began a course on commitment by asking my students to write an essay on the subject: "To whom and/or to what are you committed?" Both the students and I were disappointed with the results. It proved surprisingly difficult for them to dredge up and explain in objectifiable terms what had become organic to their lives.

37

It seemed like trying to describe a flower by exhuming it to see its roots. The assumption of my question was that commitments are definable and objectifiable, and that assumption proved to be not altogether true. One of the problems was that the self seemed to be either left out of the inquiry altogether, or it was made the whole focus of what one was committed to. To ignore the self seemed to the students to be unsound and unreal, since it is an inalienable part of one's commitment. But by the same token, to make the entire framework of commitment revolve around the self seemed both self-centered and inaccurate.

By posing a question which the students found virtually impossible to answer, I came to realize something important about the nature of commitment. The question implied that one's commitments are or can be made wholly conscious, that they are an eyes-open kind of thing —in other words, that they can be brought into the full light of day. I no longer believe this. What I am sure of is that what one is conscious of with regard to commitments is symbolic of the deeper direction one has chosen to take in one's life. The symbols I am referring to are the commitments that are formally made and the actions that are undertaken as a result of the formal commitments one has made. These actions and these formal commitments are like whitecaps, however; they are merely the most visible portion of the deeper currents and flow of one's life. The dynamism that produces our primary and secondary commitments is largely below the surface of one's consciousness and can never be fully plumbed. The full meaning of a person's commitments, therefore, must include this deeper level, for this is the direction we have chosen to go in, notwithstanding its indefinability. The contents of this deeper level are prethematic and the consciousness operating in it is prereflexive. We will call this level of commitment, this dynamism from which our conscious commitments arise, the primordial level of our commitments, or, for the sake of brevity, our primordial commitment.

The thrust one gives one's being, the way one chooses to face reality to pursue the fullness one sees oneself capable of, this is what I mean by primordial commitment. Though not fully extricable, this is where our moral responsibility reposes, par excellence. The fullness I am referring to might be conceived of by one person in terms of meaning, by someone with a different temperament in terms of love, by another person in terms of goodness or justice or beauty, etc. This primordial commitment is not *to* something nor is it to oneself; it is, however, *of* oneself in the direction in which one perceives a transcendent good. Since we are talking about the primordial flow of one's being, commitment in this fuller sense is more "felt into" than made. It is more tendential than volitional, though it is chosen. It is more discovered than made, and it is discovered only gradually. The conscious objects which symbolize it at any given moment do not exhaust it or fully express it. And they can change.

The primordial commitment, as I have described it, approximates the fundamental moral option that St. Thomas Aquinas sees as standing at the beginning of the person's moral life. Although similar, the primordial commitment differs from this fundamental option, as I perceive it, in several ways. For one, it gives direction to more than a person's moral activity. In addition, it builds only slowly over the course of a person's life. The acts of conscious formal commitment symbolize for oneself and others the direction one is taking. These conscious commitments, in turn, make the primordial commitment more explicit. They bring the direction one is taking closer to consciousness.

There is a notion contributed by psychology which is akin to, and can help to clarify the meaning of, the primordial commitment. This notion, which is called "intentionality," has been developed at some length by Rollo May.[1] His development sheds further light onto the necessarily obscure notion of primordial commitment. According to May, the intentionality of our being underlies all of our intentions. It is prior to and undergirds all of our decisions. One's intentionality is the direction one is going in. It is one's response to the structure of one's world. It determines the experiences we have, and to some extent, gives them the meaning we tend to impose upon them.

May's interest in this idea came about as a result of extensive clinical experience. His interest in spelling out the role that intentionality plays in a person's life is due to his desire to have psychoanalysis focus its own purposes more clearly. (He thinks its role should be to help a person clarify his intentionality.) May sees intentionality more in terms of the tendency of a person's life rather than that which is explicitly volitional in a person's life. That fact does not lessen the person's responsibility to bring to fuller consciousness, insofar as that is possible, his or her intentionality. He would see the individual's responsibility being exercised to the extent that one exerts oneself to plumb this dimension of one's being. In terms of

[1] Rollo May, op. cit., esp. pp. 223–45.

40

Components of Commitment

commitment, I believe May would put it this way: The problem isn't whether to commit myself to this or that, or to commit myself at all, but to discover what the flow of my being already is and, having seen that, to choose this or that direction more consciously or reject it now with greater freedom and greater awareness. Since one's intentionality includes objects of conscious choice, the question arises as to whether this or that conscious object of choice is expressive of and organic with the flow of one's intentionality, or whether it is not. If it is not, then something has to be changed. To discern the direction of one's life more fully is to know oneself and to be more realistic about oneself. To direct one's intentionality is more perfect than to be unaware of it.

By unearthing this deeper level of commitment and by giving attention to the subterranean reality of our intentionality, we have complemented our initial observation about commitment, namely that it is inextricably a part of the mystery of the person. Since our primary and secondary commitments are only a part of a much deeper reality, and since that reality is essentially impenetrable (even by the person himself), the phenomenon of human commitment has all the credentials it needs to be classified a mystery. This is important for several reasons. If one's commitments are not fully penetrable by the person himself, then they are certainly beyond the pale of another's judgments. Secondly, and even more assuredly, they should also be beyond determinations of them from without. Thirdly, the person who is attempting to resolve questions about commitment for himself should not focus exclusively on the level of conscious choice but should seek to understand the dynamism and flow that underlie his behavior patterns. Although this subterranean layer is not fully exhumable, the more aware of it one is, the freer and truer to oneself will be one's decisions about commitments.

Finally, the mystery dimension of our commitments suggests their ultimate import. In religious terms, I think they are signs of whether one is coming within range of salvation or damnation. The former is likely if one's choices are creating something beyond oneself, namely interpersonal communion. The latter is likely if one refuses to be otherwards, in presence at least of love. In other words, reductively a person's primordial commitment can flow in only one of two directions. If one's behavior is one of self-donation, one is likely to save what one is giving, i.e., oneself. If one's behavior, on the other hand, shows no signs of this but appears to be self-absorbing, one is likely to lose what one is trying to hold on to.

I should mention in this connection that is seems to me that all of our impersonal commitments (to projects, organizations, goals, ideologies, etc.) must be subordinated to interpersonal commitments if the process of self-donation is to prove self-transcending and, therefore, salvific. A life devoted exclusively to things will make a thing out of a person. These last two points should become clearer in the upcoming chapters.

THE HORIZON ONE FACES INTO

Just as a person's commitment is deeper than he can articulate, so also it is broader. Our explorations into the nature of commitment need to go into the question not only of their depth but also of their breadth. The horizon analysis of the philosophical theologians suggests a way of doing this. One's primordial commitment faces one into a horizon. This horizon gives one a field of vision which opens out to a number of possibilities and closes out others. The horizon we are facing into is the source of the potential objects of one's conscious formal commitments, both primary and secondary. Just as every primordial commitment frames the parameters of one's horizon, so also every conscious commitment is a specification of the horizon that looms before one. Each of these conscious commitments contracts the horizon and deepens it.

Unstoppable as time itself, one's horizon recedes as one proceeds. At any one moment, the realities which are in the forefront of our consciousness might seem exhaustive, but as time goes on, it becomes obvious they do not represent all of the virtualities of one's existence. Some things are too distant at any one time to be within the range of our perceptions. Other things can cause us to lose perspective if focused on exclusively.

There are several ways by which the proper interaction between one's conscious commitments and one's horizon can become disharmonious. One can "sin" by excess and become brittle or fanatic, or one can "sin" by defect. We will deal with overcommitment, that is with the former situation, at the end of the chapter. With regard to the latter, the failure to make commitments, or to neglect following through with those already made, leaves a person with the burden of shallowness. One cannot sacrifice depth in the interests of breadth without finding that breadth rapidly becomes problematical. In other words, when the primordial commitment does not have adequate symbols to flesh out its direction, superficiality, or identity diffusion, is an inevitable consequence.

Can there be a qualitative shift in one's horizon? That is to say, can a former horizon be abandoned and a new one embraced? The answer to this obviously is that there can be because there is. One need merely think of the many conversion stories one hears, whether religious or philosophical or whatever. One need think only of the "defections" (so-called) one hears about daily; these show up when there are withdrawals from previously cherished positions, previous spouses, previous ways of life, previous life styles. Horizon shifts are of considerable importance to the question of commitment because new horizons create new commitments and frequently strain or cause former commitments to be discarded. Many of the commitment problems which arise relate directly to the question of whether or not one was right in yielding to the new horizon one has accepted. Frequently this is the moment for the question to be asked, not when one begins to wonder about one's commitments after this new horizon has been accepted.

The reason we call this a horizon shift is because one's previous perspective is transcended. This means that the whole way one perceived reality, the principles and judgments one took to deal with the reality one found oneself in, has changed. I use the word "transcended" not in the sense that all horizon shifts are necessarily from the less good to the better or from the less true to the more true, but only in the sense that the previous stance is no longer where one is now standing to perceive reality. I say "shift" because we are not to confuse a horizon shift with the natural evolution that all horizons undergo. Being human, one becomes, and in the course of becoming, one's horizons evolve; our perspectives evolve—or at least they should. A horizon shift is more radical than the natural evolution of a person's horizon.

The breakthrough from the old to the new can come at the level of one's emotions, one's mind or one's values. It can be religious, affective, or intellectual. It can be a combination of all of these but with one of them predominant. It can be somewhat organic to, and in continuity with, the previous horizon, or it can be an abrupt and radical departure from the previous state. Sometimes the freedom one feels about his choice of the new horizon seems minimal, since whatever stimulated the breakthrough was compelling and as abrupt as it was unexpected. At other times, the shift is more gradual. The new horizon might be mediated by any number of things: a person, a special grace, a tragedy, a teacher, an ideological breakthrough, or an unexpected event in one's life or in society. New commitments are made and others discarded because of the shift. The same commitments could be kept, of course, though they would have to be realigned, given the new horizon.

A person is not a passive observer of a new horizon—or at least he should not be. He can pursue it, ratify it, accept it, or turn away and reject it. What one should do about such a shift is a complex question. The new horizon will always present itself under some aspect as good. In some way it will purport to be truer, or more relevant, or deeper, or more beautiful, or more just than the one that presently obtains in one's life. Since one is often relatively passive at the dawning of a new horizon, its acceptance is something else, something about which a decision must be made. (We are assuming that the acceptance of the new horizon, like its rejection, is a free act.)

A distinction is germane at this point between horizontal freedom and vertical freedom. The distinction comes from Joseph de Finance, the Belgian philosopher.[2] The exercise of freedom within a given horizon concentrates on the objects which present themselves in this specifiable context. Within those parameters one's choices and commitments are made with what De Finance calls horizontal freedom. If a new horizon is to be accepted—that is to say, if one chooses to yield to heretofore unexpected parameters—one must accept with this new horizon all that this implies for the future, and about the past. When the person chooses to make the new horizon his own, he is exercising what De Finance refers to as a vertical act of freedom.

It is obvious why this distinction is relevant to a study on commitment. Many changes of commitment come about because of a prior exercise of vertical freedom. The person's whole *Weltanschauung* has changed, maybe gradually, maybe abruptly, but radically in either case. Because of this, he may appear to be consistent to himself, given this new horizon, by withdrawing from his previous commitments and choosing new symbols more apt to express himself and inconsistent to everyone else who does not appreciate the radical change in perspective he has undergone. The problematic moment is the moment in which the new horizon was acceded to. The legitimacy of that yielding is, therefore, the more serious question, rather than the particular follow-through or what one does with regard to this or that commitment. If there has been a shift of horizon, concern with and discernment

2 Cf. Bernard Lonergan, *Method in Theology* (New York: Herder and Herder, 1972), pp. 40 and 237.

46

about commitments, without regard to the decision about the horizon change, focuses on a symptom, not a cause. The misfocus augurs poorly for any discernment that will result from this.

In general, there are three different ways in which breakthroughs to new horizons occur in people's lives, though they are not altogether separable. It could be primarily in the area of meaning that the new horizon comes about. When this is the case, one's future judgments will be made according to different principles than those which were operative before. For example, a conversion to Marxism would drastically change one's economic principles, possibly one's ethical and political convictions, and probably one's religious standards and values, with the result that all subsequent choices and commitments would be assumed in terms of this new horizon of meaning. The crucial moment for such a potential horizon change is the moment of judgment about its truth. This judgment is usually a free one in the sense that the evidence will not be so overwhelmingly convincing by itself that one is coerced into embracing a new horizon. In other words, sometimes one must will it as well as see it, or will it in order to see it. I think that this is generally true of radical changes in the meaning systems people embrace in life.

Another horizon shift could be primarily one of value, although obviously this is not wholly dissociable from the above. The new value would have been either ignored in the previous horizon or given considerably less attention. The horizon shift that takes place in women who can fully subscribe to the new value of liberation would be a case in point. Marriages already undertaken either break under the impact or are forced to undergo a process of differentiation which allows the new horizon free rein. The value matrix lived in before will now be seen as obsolescent or too angular and will be discarded. All conscious object commitments, therefore, will eventually have to be realigned in view of this new perception; if not realigned, then jettisoned. Once again, the crucial judgment that has to be made pertains, first of all, to the basic value that the new horizon proffers, rather than on all judgments and decisions that are consequent upon this.

A third way for horizons to change comes from what appears to be a religious experience, a conversion. The conversion might be a passage from nonbelief to belief or, more often, from belief to a new degree of awareness of God, or a new understanding of God's love, or a new vision of the implications of the religion one has previously embraced. Obviously, a religious conversion can also be illusory, a subscribing to a bogus vision based on a misunderstood or imagined experience. The same factors obtain as in the previous two examples. One is being asked to exercise an act of vertical freedom, and the truth of the new horizon must be determined on the basis of the authenticity or inauthenticity of the purported religious experience in which this new horizon dawned.

The reader should recall in this connection "the Pauline privilege" passage in I Corinthians 7:12–15. It is enlightening insofar as it acknowledges that a (religious) horizon shift has taken place, and it suggests norms for the conduct of the already married Christian toward his or her spouse. "If a brother has a wife who is an unbeliever, and she is content to live with him, he must not send her away" (v. 12). The same goes for the wife whose husband

is an unbeliever. "She must not leave him" if he is content
with the new horizon that has opened out to her (v. 13).
In other words, stick with the old commitment even
though one's conversion has given one a qualitatively
different perspective on life than one had before. But Paul
goes on: "If, however, the unbelieving partner does not
consent, they may separate; in these circumstances the
brother or sister is not tied: God has called you to a life of
peace" (v. 15). Paul says, if realignment does not work
and the conversion is authentic, the bond one previously
entered into no longer holds.

INDWELLING

The breakthrough into the new horizon, finally, may
come about first and foremost at the level of one's affec-
tivity or emotions. The classic case here, of course, is the
person who falls in love. The beloved can exert such an
effect that one comes to see everything in a new light;
hence, the propriety of describing this experience as a horizon change. Through the eyes of the beloved, as it were,
a different world dawns. I do not want to give the impres-
sion that I think falling in love and being in love are a
univocal experience in any respect. On the contrary! The
difference of degree are as many as the number of loves
there are. The degree of "fall," like the depth of the "in,"
also admits of enormous variation.

The preposition *in* in the phrase "being in love" is
worth reflecting on. It correctly implies that one is no
longer where one was and that one is, as it were, envel-
oped by a new reality. But not every experience which
purports to be love is, and consequently, should not be

automatically yielded to. One who falls in love falls *from* somewhere. Where one falls from, and why, cannot be disregarded if one is sincerely seeking to discern the rightness or wrongness of the new horizon one is attracted to. One must ask oneself, therefore, why one was predisposed to fall. Was it because one neglected the relationship or relationships most immediate to one prior to falling? Or had those relationships shown themselves intrinsically inadequate and impoverishing, through no fault of one's own? Falling in love is a disruptive experience, among other things, and one cannot justify the disruption if it is preceded by negligence or a failure in justice or love to those with whom one is already linked. On the other hand, one cannot but welcome such an experience if it happens to those whose lives, through no fault of their own, have been relatively barren. Obviously, the issue cannot be decided merely on the basis of the so-called chemistry that is involved. The chemistry factor makes the new experience neither good nor bad, only intense and needing a decision.

By comparison, the communion question is a considerably more important consideration. By communion here I mean the matrix of relationships which circumscribe one's life. The quality of the communion one had with others before such an experience and the communion one is entering into (if one can project oneself trustworthily into the future) must be taken into account. Horizon questions of this nature, like all commitment questions, should not be solved in the context of "I am" but only in the context of "we are," as we will see in the next chapter.

Let us assume at this point that the disruptive experience of falling in love has been seen to be right and good for the persons involved and, therefore, is yielded to. Rather than inquiring further into this new existential situation as a horizon shift, we will concentrate on the experience of "indwelling" which can come about as a result of falling in love. By "indwell" I mean that the entire reality of the person has moved from being to being-in-love. The person no longer faces into his or her horizon as a solitary but, to some degree, feels, thinks, plans, and acts from within the new existential reality of being-in-love. Love of the other has one leave oneself to indwell the new context which mutual love has created.

There are different levels and different kinds of indwelling. The most frequent instance is of a man and woman in marriage, but we should not limit its possibilities to this. Jesus obviously believed indwelling could take place between himself and his followers, even though on the night he indicated his desire for it he was aware that he was going to his death. "Make your home in me, as I make mine in you . . . Whoever remains in me, with me in him, bears fruit in plenty" (John 15:4–5). Indwelling, in other words, can be intramundane or between God and human beings. It can also take place at great depth between two persons who do not relate to one another in a sexual way. In fact, the best description I have read of the experience of indwelling was written by Gregory of Nazianzen concerning his friendship with Saint Basil:

> It seemed as though there were but one soul between us, having two bodies. And if we must not believe those who

say that all things are in all things, yet you must believe this, that we were both in each one of us, and the one in the other . . .[3]

How does being-in-love, or indwelling, relate to commitment?

A) I suspect that the image we have of indwelling operates as a paradigm by which we measure the value of all commitments, both the ones we have made and those that might be made but which do not yet exist. This paradigm does not operate in a fully conscious manner, but I believe it does operate, nonetheless, since indwelling the reality of love is the milieu we were made for and seek. Being-in-love completes being and is its *raison d'être*. Until we get there our dissatisfaction will make us feel that we are not yet where we want to be.

B) For many, the image they have of indwelling will be of a marriage, but not necessarily their own. It could be a potential union, marital in form, imaged and idealized and made into a paradigm to measure all other commitments. This spousal image certainly does not exclude God's relationship with human beings or our commitment to God, since the Hebrew and Christian Scriptures explicitly refer to the potential indwelling between the two in spousal imagery.

C) Other uses of the word "commitment" are, I think, analogous to, and spinoffs from, this prime analogue and paradigm of indwelling.

D) The disruptive experience of falling in love will not proceed into a condition of being-in-love if a commitment

[3] Quoted by William Johnston, *Silent Music* (New York: Harper & Row, Publishers, 1974), p. 144.

is not forthcoming. That is to say, the relationship must be formally and fully chosen and pass beyond the spontaneous attraction for each other.

E) The ideal condition for the living-out of an interpersonal commitment is for it to take place within the existential reality of indwelling.

The experience of being-in-love need not be disruptive of one's prior commitments. It can, in fact, prove to be a source of rejuvenation for them. In some cases, it can be the first indication of what has been previously wanting in the living-out of one's previous commitments. More concretely, an unusual friendship which flowers into indwelling can bring to a previous relationship hitherto unsuspected depths. Though rare, an individual may be in love with someone other than his or her spouse and, at the same time, find that this indwelling is the instrument through which the spousal relationship is renewed. (Admittedly, the number of times in which this does not happen and prior commitments are discarded by one or both parties is infinitely greater than the number of times in which it does happen. When one's prior primary commitments are not reinforced by this new experience of indwelling, chances are good that the love which inspired the latter relationship was bogus.) In other words, it is conceivable that a friendship can flower into the degree of love we call indwelling and yet enjoy only a secondary status in the order of one's commitments because of the prior, primary commitments of one or all of the parties concerned. If the indwelling is authentic, it will serve to give these primary commitments new life.

It is obvious that far too few primary commitments have been generated by the force of love, and fewer still are lived-out from within the experience of indwelling. This does not mean that they cannot be or that they will never be. By being "faithful over a few things" and by living in hope, indwelling can develop. The catalyst for bringing long-standing relationships that are rooted in commitments to which one has been faithful but which have not developed into the existential reality of indwelling, is frequently enough a third party. (Admittedly, this is said with great caution because of the risk of breaking primary commitments, but since indwelling is the milieu needed for personhood to develop, much more can be lost by aprioristically closing oneself off from any "outside" relationships. I am not baptizing a form of "open marriage" here, but, because I believe in marriage, I am pointing to the ability of friendship to strengthen in some cases the bond between husband and wife.) This applies in turn to many other interpersonal situations in which a commitment grown stale can be rejuvenated by a new experience of the power of love from outside.

The surest sign that love is operating in a situation which purports to be one of indwelling is that it shows itself inclusive of those to whom one is already linked and that it accepts and reinforces the identity and life situation each has chosen for himself prior to the indwelling. It will never be successful if either party fails to bring back what each is becoming as a result of the new experience of indwelling, to the one (or to the community in the case of religious etc.) with whom one has shared one's becoming and with whom one is joined in commitment. Indwelling is a dynamic reality that cannot remain long at the intimistic stage that involves only two parties. It must flower into, and become part of, a larger communion.

54

OVERCOMMITMENT

As was mentioned in a previous section, one can "sin" by defect or by excess in this matter of commitment. By defect, I mean that one can either be unaware of any conscious objects that symbolize the primordial flow of one's being, or one can be so anemically committed to whomever or whatever that one's commitments exert no appreciable pull in one's life. Even though one might be in what, viewed from outside, appears to be a commitment situation, in fact no self-donation is taking place. One is self-absorbed.

The question arises from the opposite end of the spectrum: Can one be overcommitted? Obviously one can have too many commitments and forfeit the possibility of being a free and integrated human being for that reason. But the overcommitment I have in mind here is of a different sort. It occurs when people pursue a commitment so exclusively that their lives become brittle and their horizons narrow. By overcommitment, I mean the investing of more of the self in the object of one's commitment than the object can or should deliver. This kind of overcommitment is much more socially destructive than noncommitment. No one who lives in the twentieth century can be oblivious of the fact that the history of all of us has been shaped all too frequently by the overcommitment of the few. Every fanatic is overcommitted, though not every overcommitment makes one a fanatic. The unfreedom which is associated in the minds of many with commitment is usually the result of what overcommitment does in people. And many times what looks like the betrayal of a commitment is actually a long-overdue with-drawal from an unhealthy overcommitment.

The one guilty of overcommitment places the object—a position, an organization, an ideology, a vocation, or what-ever—in a position where it is asked to perform the func-tions of integration and direction and meaning, of identity almost, that the person alone should bear responsibility for. One loses all perspective; the object of one's commit-ment becomes all-consuming; one's identity merges into rather than develops from the commitment. One is not conscious of this, of course, at the time the commitment is made. That one is guilty of, or will be the victim of, over-commitment—that is to say, of oversubscribing one's self-hood to an object—will occur to one only in time, if at all.

Some examples are in order here. Reflect on the number of marriages in which one of the partners is for all pratical purposes asked to supply a personality and identity to the other. The result of such a union is the virtual obliteration of the distinctiveness of one of the partners. (In the past, this seems to have been more prevalent with females than with males.) To entertain unreal expectations of the other or the state of marriage in general, to hope to establish a sense of self-worth and personal identity through it or through the other, is the precondition for overcommit-ment. After such a marriage takes place, what the spouses need is liberation not from their partner but from their overcommitment, their demand that the other be what each one alone can become.

It is commonplace, on the other hand, to see the Ameri-can male become a victim of his own overcommitment to his occupation or his profession. The need for position or power or a sense of accomplishment or achievement is a precondition for his overcommitment. Ideological over-commitment also abounds. Such is the case when a person takes a few ideas and makes them absolute, embraces them emotionally, and applies them to reality, claiming that the true is what he or she sees and the untrue is what everyone else sees, the true is what he or she thinks and the untrue is what everyone else thinks. And finally, institutional overcommitment is also prevalent. Who does not know people whose life has virtually become a place, or an institution, to such a degree that they would fall apart if they were removed from it?

Some of the clinical evidence for the phenomenon of overcommitment comes from the well-known psychologist Eric Erikson.[4] The object of one of his studies was adolescents whose commitments come about because of their need to give themselves to something or someone to whom they can pledge their loyalty. Their overcommitment comes about because they subscribed to the mystique and ideology, as Erikson calls it, with which the object of their commitment was surrounded either by the adolescent's own imagination or by the religious, social, or political institution that evoked their commitment.

The reasons for overcommitment, whether in adolescents or in adults, are several. Recall another psychologist, Abraham Maslow, and his distinctions between growth needs and deficiency needs. Some interpersonal commitments are an attempt to supply for deficiency needs. They will never be successful as long as that is the driving force that has brought them into being. Our commitments to others should come from our own growth needs; other-

[4] E. H. Erikson, *Insight and Responsibility* (New York: W. W. Norton & Co., Inc., 1964), pp. 125ff.

wise, we are liable to use others to make up for and compensate for what we cannot ourselves supply.

Once one tries to divest oneself of the anguish of personal search and self-discovery in this way, one will be guilty of using commitment to avoid personal search and decision and risk and discovery. These must continue throughout life; one cannot make someone else responsible for oneself. Anytime the other or the object of one's commitment is being burdened with and made responsible for the self, we are in the area of overcommitment.

Overcommitment can also stem from a lack of faith in God or from a faith one has allowed to become anemic. Such a person seeks to wrest from a creature or a finite reality something which only God can supply. Clothing the object of his commitment with ultimacy, he creates a situation which can only bring about tension and frustration for himself and eventually for others. Paul Tillich in his *Dynamics of Faith* describes instances of this and the resultant suicides that so many members of the Third Reich were propelled to after the fall of Nazism. They had invested the ideology of Hitler with ultimacy, or, to put it in more religious terms, they put something considerably less than the kingdom of God first and adorned it with kingdom credentials, and eventually it and all other things were taken away from them as a result. Any object of our commitments, except when that object is God himself, can become a source of overcommitment when it ceases to be finite and postures as the ultimate good of our being.

Although the blame for overcommitment most often belongs to the individual, in some cases it can also be traced to the group. There are not a few instances in

58

Components of Commitment

which the group's need for allegiance is the source of the problem, and the reason why overcommitments are elicited by the group. The atmosphere in which such overcommitments are generated is usually one of isolation in which there is an uncritical trust in the myths that the group has embraced or in the authority figures that the group has installed.

This aspect of the subject of overcommitment has been handled with much imagination by the Stony Brook sociologist Lewis A. Coser. Although he exaggerates many of his points and misunderstands both the Roman Catholic Church and the Society of Jesus, he does advance some interesting evidence to show how many institutions of society can rightly be described as greedy. From their members "they seek exclusive and undivided loyalty and they attempt to reduce the claims of competing roles and status positions on those they wish to encompass within their boundaries. Their demands on the person are omnivorous."[5] According to Coser, one of the chief means they use to persuade people to overcommit themselves to them is the regulation of sexual attachments, so that members will devote their total energies to the collective tasks the institutions have decided upon.

What should be done, once overcommitment is diagnosed as the victimizing culprit in one's life? Sometimes perception itself can remedy the condition. Simple recognition of the false expectations one has entertained about the object of one's commitment can often enable one to get on with the job of living. Or one can begin a process

[5] Lewis A. Coser, *Greedy Institutions* (New York: The Free Press, 1974), p. 4. My general complaint with the book is that it fails to see the positive values of commitment, so focused is the author on the evil of institutions that elicit overcommitments from people.

of differentiation within oneself and realignment of one's commitment to the primordial flow of one's being. Or, finally, one can withdraw from the initial commitment completely. In brief, overcommitment is as inimical to growth as no commitment at all, and the sooner the condition is perceived the sooner growth into freedom through commitment can take place.

In this chapter we have examined several of the more important components of interpersonal commitments. We have seen that this aspect of a person's life lies deeper than the objects to which he is consciously committed whether these be personal or impersonal. In turn, we looked at the horizon of possibilities every person faces into because it is within this horizon that the objects of one's commitments are discovered. The freedom of choice that is exercised can be horizontal or vertical, depending on whether what is inviting our assent is organic to or discontinuous with the previous horizon. Our commitments will be accordingly affected especially when the new horizon is being mediated by a person with whom one is in love. Finally, we saw that the bad press commitment is saddled with is often due to the excessive investment people at times make in the objects of their commitments.

Chapter III
The Problematic of Permanence

Most people readily affirm the value of commitment. Their personal difficulty with it relates not to commitment itself, but with the quality of permanence that some commitments are supposed to have. This lifelong quality is proving to be the point at which the ideal, if that is what it is, is disintegrating. We need not bring forward a pile of sociological data to prove this point. Even the most unreflective observer would have to admit that lifelong commitments do not last for life in these our days. Hence, the need to examine the factor of permanence in commitment.

If the promise of forever is becoming as obsolete as the covered wagon, which at times it looks like it is, the question we must ask ourselves is whether we should just accept that and continue the charade of promising "forever" while meaning "for now." Or, if it can be established that there is an intrinsic connection between permanence and at least some commitments, then we should be less ready

61

to accept the transiency and impermanence of so many contemporary commitments.

On the face of it, it seems that there is an intrinsic connection between "forever" and some commitments. The most convincing way that people have hit upon to state the fact that they are not placing conditions on the giving of themselves to another is to confess that they are not setting a predetermined time span within which the relationship is to work. In other words, the most congenial way we humans have of showing that our commitments are unconditional is to say "forever." Granted this is a resort to quantity terms in order to prove quality, but who has found a better way to express total commitment to another person than to say that we include him or her in our entire future?

Apart from the intention of permanence and apart from the fact that the forms of most vows profess "forever," what is the justification for so total and irrevocable a disposition of one's life? I believe the justification for this kind of human behavior comes down to this: A better way of growing has not been discovered than to put down roots. Adolescence is a time of inevitable, if awkward, growth. The physical, emotional, and intellectual aspects of the individual cannot but grow. It is a time of disengagement from the family. It is a period of diffusion; possibilities are many but disjointed; energy is dispersed in a zigzag way. One has to be an adolescent for a while; one shouldn't be an adolescent for long. One can remain an adolescent throughout life, however. The perpetual adolescent withholds himself, refusing to put down roots. He dabbles with life rather than living it.

The parable of the sower suggests that the business of

putting down roots admits of a variety of depths. The yield one produces in life can run anywhere from an immature seed size to an abundant hundredfold harvest. The difference will be due largely to the use, nonuse, or abuse one makes of the word "forever." The intention of the planter in giving his word, plus the ground one's words falls on are two of the variables that cause the outcome to differ so greatly. Which is to say, some permanent commitments lack depth because of the person who makes them. Others, because of the context which has received them. If the intention of the one making the commitment is timid and tentative, then when difficulties arise, the superficiality of the roots will be exposed.

Or the problem could be with the soil, which is to say, the context within which the commitment was made. It could be too cluttered and incapable of sufficiently nurturing the commitment made. Or it might be rich *and* the intention of both parties profound, but the result will still be sadly wanting. Competing allegiances, the clutter of too many secondary commitments, inconsistency about priorities, inability to order one's life according to clearly seen priorities—these and any number of other factors can inhibit the growth of the seeds from reaching thirty, sixty, or a hundredfold. But there are those who have given their word, whose lives show the fruit of a permanent commitment. They need no justification for the totality of their self-gift. It authenticates itself. The most convincing evidence of the value of the irrevocable disposition of one's life must always be in the fruit that it produces. By contrast, one can reflect on the effect on those who have withheld themselves throughout life from self-donation.

Of itself, a permanent commitment is not more perfect than a temporary commitment. A permanent commitment is justified only if the object of one's commitment is consonant with fulfilling the transcendent end each person is capable of attaining. But the only "objects" that can measure up to this qualification are persons (and the personal God). It is traditional wisdom to see that the only way a person fulfills himself is by transcending himself. And the most efficacious way a person can get outside and beyond himself is through another person—through love of another person, to be more exact. Self-transcendence through self-donation, in a word.

It follows from this that love is the only justification for the permanent disposition of one's life. Love is the only intentionality that warrants the outlay of one's total self. Only in love can the needs and capacities of human beings be fulfilled. Any commitment dynamic that intends permanence and yet fails to flow from love, or at least give promise of leading to love, will prove to be a deterrent to growth and transcendence.

Commitment is the most natural way of both expressing the love one has for another (the Other) and of proving as well as preserving that same love. All other things being equal, permanence will be a property of every commitment that flows from love and continues in love. Permanence in interpersonal relationships, if built on anything less than love or the aspiration to love, can be cruel to all parties concerned. This will be the inevitable result if social stability or social acceptance is the only reason for the liaison's continuance. Permanence all too often becomes a rack upon which persons are torturously twisted, either by their own consciences or by those to whom they have made a commitment, or by third parties (family, one's children, society, church). Holding someone to an interpersonal commitment because he has made a contract whose terms must be observed is an inhuman way of maintaining the social order.

If the loving remains, the permanence of the commitment is assured. But loving involves many different acts. One of them is a kind of dying. There must be continual vigilance to avoid reverting to the kind of thinking of oneself and solitary acting and planning that characterized one's life before the commitment. More picturesquely, the grain of wheat must choose again and again the selfsame soil in which it was first embedded. It is at the point of commitment that a person is both rising out of self-absorption into a fuller life and yet dying to a solitary mode of being.

What is the precise nature of the dying that a commitment entails? One of the best understandings of commitment I have seen has been able to excise the key ethical characteristic that makes a commitment a commitment, and, therefore, as I see it, reveals the kind of dying a commitment entails.[1] The key ethical characteristic of a commitment is the claim one yields to another over oneself with regard to one's future. Sister Margaret Farley indicates that in a commitment we enter a relationship "wherein we are bound to future free actions because we have entrusted something of ourselves to another on the basis of which that other has a claim on our action."[2] One of her study's conclusions: ". . . our analysis of commitment has led us to recognize a ground of obligation not in

[1] Sister Margaret A. Farley, op. cit., esp. pp. 50–89.
[2] Ibid., p. 78.

SHOULD ANYONE SAY FOREVER?

a law of the will, nor in a free choice which is not thereby limited, nor in a fiction which facilitates enlightened self-interest, but in the being of the person of the other, to whom we commit ourselves."[3]

As long as the commitment maintains this other-regarding characteristic, permanence will not be problematical. But should the "grain of wheat" come to focus on itself, and the cost of the commitment and the dying that is involved, then permanence becomes problematical. Permanence and the cost involved in commitment are both self-regarding notions. They take the focus off of the other and the experience of the other that brought the commitment into being, and rivet it on oneself. Just as one can hardly intend the "dying" that a commitment involves in and of itself, so also one can hardly intend permanence in and of itself. Both must be consequences of the love that generates the commitment.

It is natural to attempt to invest with the quality of permanence what we have found to be good—that is, a relationship in which some measure of indwelling takes place. And so we use the word "forever" when we have found what or whom we wish to be in union with time without end. "Forever" describes the disposition one makes of one's future, at least insofar as one's intention can determine the future. "Forever" is more than an apt way of expressing the quality of unconditional love; it also expresses an aspiration for permanence. I say "aspiration" because at no one point does permanence become an accomplished fact. Nothing human is permanent.

"Forever" should not express an aspiration to persevere "come what may," but an aspiration to become together

[3] Ibid., p. 309.

come what may. What is inimical to permanent commitments is fixity, which is to say, the failure to become. What makes a permanent commitment work is that one becomes and yet one does not change one's intention to become together, or to share one's becoming with the other. This does not necessarily mean that one's becoming must always take place directly with the person or the community to whom one is committing oneself. The commitment implies that one will "bring" one's becoming to the other, not that this becoming will always take place together.

THE ROOTS OF OUR AMBIGUITY ABOUT PERMANENCE

I think we are all a bit muddled about permanence. We seem to do our best to try to escape it, while we spend our lifetime yearning for it. We dread the thought of being locked into something irrevocable. At the same time, we yearn for permanent bliss and security. Think of the years spent in hard labor by so many people so that they can be financially secure in their final years. And the fact that believers bank their whole lives on the state of permanent bliss we call heaven should tell us something about our ambivalence. Are not our aspirations for permanence summed up in this prayer for the deceased we love and pray for: "Eternal rest grant unto them, O Lord, and let perpetual light shine upon them!"?

There are a number of reasons why we are muddled about the subject of permanence. One has to do with the images it conjures up. Another has to do with the social conditions of modern life which pervasively bespeak transiency. And a third has to do with our cultural past.

The images we tend to associate with permanency can be counterproductive to commitment. The image a permanent commitment suffers from is that it is a once-and-for-all-time choice. This doesn't accurately reflect the behavior of people. A once-and-for-all-time choice is rare, and what is even more rare is a successful once-and-for-all-time choice. A permanent commitment is much more likely to be successful if it is an unconditional choice or, better, a principle of choice so that every conscious rechoosing is a renewal of the original commitment. Since "forever" connotes fixity, it is not surprising that many resist committing themselves fully, for it seems to imply that one is making a decision to stop living or growing or becoming. While permanence seems to be a threat to spontaneity, it could and should have the opposite effect. It should foster spontaneity. Once one's life has taken a definitive direction, one should be more, not less, capable of growth. For among other things, people will know where one stands and can begin to relate more deeply to the person. The individual ceases to be ambiguous; he is coming *from* somewhere, so growth for him builds on the strengths already accumulated. Since one's life is rooted, growth can be expected, as fruit is expected only from a plant that is rooted.

Another reason for our ambiguity is the social conditions within which our commitments are made or resisted, persevered in or broken. These conditions seem increasingly to foster and to favor transiency. The three social conditions that lent a degree of rootedness and permanence to man's life in the past are rapidly disappearing. I'm referring to rootedness to one place, lifelong performance of one skill, and the stability of clan-centered rela-

68

tionships. Reflect, by way of contrast, on the bewildering mobility of modern Americans. The U. S. Department of Labor estimates that Americans in their mid-twenties can expect six or seven major job changes in the course of their working years. In addition, consider the high degree of transiency in human relationships; and one can begin to appreciate the external factors that affect the whole meaning and possibility of personal commitment.

Not that living things haven't always undergone change. They have. What is new is the rapidity of it. Just reflect on the forms within which permanent commitments are made. I am thinking primarily of marriage, ministry, and religious life. The changes in understanding and practice that each of these forms has undergone, especially in the last fifteen years, are unprecedented. No one in these "states" of life can be unaffected by changes within their peculiar form of commitment. Each person is subject to the pressure and tension of change within the very form (ironically) which expressed his or her permanent commitment.

Instead of making permanent commitment passé, it seems to me that all of these new social conditions only add to the urgency of the question. Caught in the swirl of a throwaway culture, more and more people are wondering how to create for themselves a life situation that gives promise of stability.

The third source of our ambiguity comes from our history, whether cultural, intellectual or religious. Esteem for permanence in human commitments is part of our heritage as Christians and as Westerners. It is a part of our heritage that is rapidly disappearing, so we had better examine this particular quality of commitment before we bid it fond adieu. We could also conclude that we ought to be doing better than we have been doing lately at preserving it.

First a glimpse at the roots of this esteem. Greek and Roman society, both civil and religious, and the cultures which succeeded them up until modern times, have prized permanence and stability. Nature itself—or the way nature was viewed, to be more precise—probably had a lot to do in forming this attitude. Our forebears saw the firmament as fixed, with the moon and sun and stars locked into their respective courses. Change occurred only in, and according to, predetermined patterns, since everything in the known universe had its fixed place, including, and especially, humans. From Aristotle on, this universe was believed to be presided over by a mysterious reality, the most estimable term for which was the Unmoved Mover. To be beyond change was to be perfect. To be subject to change was the lot of creatures. It was inevitable that changelessness would become a measure of human perfection.

The comparative immobility of society fed these beliefs, of course. The meagerness of the means of communication and travel, the ubiquity of self-sustaining agricultural skills, and the omnipresence of natural resources —all these factors tended to make for stability, rather than mobility, of domicile, occupation, and clan. Together, these contributed to fashioning a world view in which a serf remained a serf, a commoner a commoner, a nobleman a nobleman, etc.

Scholastic metaphysics raised this world view to a true-for-all-times philosophical position. Creatures were composed of "substances" and "accidents," and the former never changed. God was Pure Act, the Being who would not move from potency to act. Possessing all perfection, such a movement would imply imperfection and therefore call his divinity into question.

The Church reinforced with the seal of her authority the cultural esteem for permanence that her children had inherited from their respective cultures. She began to attach fixed parameters to each of the vocational forms her members chose to live in. Membership in monastic life, for instance, came to be sealed by perpetual vows. (Something unheard of in Buddhist monasteries and Hindu ashrams. The philosophical option made in Buddhist and Hindu societies was for becoming over being.) The most frequent vocational choice of Christians, of course, was marriage. It, too, took on the same character of permanence when it was determined that the marriage bond was indissoluble. In addition, it was determined that the priestly "character" of one who received Holy Orders was indelible.

The Church has unmistakably affirmed and baptized the relative immobility of the cultural experience of the past. She has made what we now see was a philosophical option, part and parcel of her self-understanding. Her predilection for that option has never been withdrawn, and is not likely to be, as we shall consider in the last chapter. The reason for her option was not merely philosophical. She has sought to mirror the fidelity of God himself in her determinations.

Meanwhile, much has happened in the world of men and things. The increasingly strong currents of modern times are all running counter to the Church's option. Process is king. Actualization of potencies and the resultant perfection are no longer part of our thought forms. Evolution is our expectation. Relativity itself is no longer a matter of dispute; only "how much?" is. Stability has been unseated by the developmental.

Some of this change came about because of social and technological developments, and some was propelled by intellectual forces. In this latter category there was Darwin and Freud, Hegel and Marx, Einstein and Whitehead; there was existentialism and the developmental methodology of the social sciences. We will deal with only one of the intellectual forces: Jean Paul Sartre.

JEAN PAUL SARTRE

We will attend to him because the fare he serves up accords perfectly with the mood and behavior of many moderns. I am not suggesting that there are a significant number of explicit Sartreans among us, but I am saying that many would develop their philosophy along Sartrean lines if they undertook the task of creating a philosophy on the basis of their own comportment in the area of commitment. Jean Paul Sartre's ideas, furthermore, should help to bring together some of the questions we have voiced about permanence in commitment. While this twentieth-century existentialist is a vigorous proponent of both freedom and commitment, he advances notions about the meaning of each of these that reconceives what previous generations had thought about them.

Sartre sees each person as driven by a "fundamental project." A person's whole being is taken up with the pursuit of this. It is fundamental because it unifies, supposedly, all of one's lesser purposes and projects. This project is so radically one with the individual's personality that Sartre is wont to refer to it as "the fundamental project which I am." It is a project in the sense that it involves the projection of one's entire self into the future. It is not permanent in the sense of having a fixed content perceived from the outset. It is, rather, a developing thing which, as he puts it, "is continually recovering the past in the pursuit of the future" and, therefore, is in constant need of renewal for that reason. What one's project is at any one time is in a constant state of potential revocation. It can be discarded "in the interests of a beyond which I shall be."

One already begins to see in these few lines of thought implications about commitment. One's fundamental project is what one is committed to. Sartre conceives this not in terms of persons but of actions. Action undertaken on behalf of people, perhaps, but the frame of reference of Sartrean commitment is not the other. His anthropology is individualistic and his conception of a commitment remains within the one making it. This can be seen by the lack of concern and attention Sartre gives to those immediately affected by the person's movement out of one fundamental project into another. He does not concern himself with the question of responsibility toward those with whom one has previously involved oneself. He concerns himself only with the freedom of the individual and his project. Is it not callous to think that others are simply standing by as so many observers while Sartrean man frees himself to go from one project to another?

As one could predict, there is an unusual notion of freedom underlying Sartre's ideas about the fundamental project. Sartre would go considerably beyond the universally acceptable idea that human beings should be self-determining. He would go so far as to say that it is only to the extent that a person is actually exercising his freedom that he is human. In his famous work *Being and Nothingness*, Sartre observed: "What we call freedom is impossible to distinguish from the being of human reality. Man does not exist first, in order to be free subsequently; there is no difference between the being of man and his being-free."[4] In Sartre's mind, freedom is conceived differently than any traditional understanding. It is close to being the creator of humanness and the source of everything we are.

In examining Sartre's notions on freedom, one has to distinguish the early Sartre from the later.[5] In the Sartre of *Being and Nothingness*, his concern was that one win freedom by escaping society's determinations. Otherwise one is merely an ornament amid other ornaments, he felt, an object submerged in the solidity of other substances. Lacking in spontaneity, one's actions then erupt from a fixed essence hemmed in by a constricting past. One must free oneself from these predeterminations. At this point in Sartre's reflections, freedom is *from* not *for;* it seeks to transcend the subordinations that society, religion, etc., would impose. He admits that this kind of freedom is "synonymous with lack," that one finds oneself facing into the void, having only anguish and uncertainty as one's companions.

The later Sartre never renounces this thesis but complements it with a Marxist one. His most important publica-

---

[4] Jean Paul Sartre, *Being and Nothingness* (New York: Washington Square Press, 1966), p. 30.
[5] I have found a fine treatment of this in Father Thomas King's *Sartre and the Sacred* (Chicago: University of Chicago Press, 1974).

74

tion in his later phase is the *Critique de la Raison Dialectique*.[6] Its emphasis is on engagement in the world. While maintaining his belief in the importance of freedom, he now stresses creative, effective action in the world of men and matter. History is to be made through praxis, which means one must plunge oneself by means of action into the muddled, complex, finite skein of men and matter. While freedom in the first place was tantamount to withdrawal, in the second phase it is seen as getting one's hands dirty through engagement. Having renounced his unity with the world of objects and thereby won his freedom, Sartrean man proceeds to the next stage of freedom—action.

Sartre never attempts a synthesis of these two meanings of freedom. They do not contradict each other, but he does little to show how they complement each other. The irony of his later ideas about freedom is that they remain individualistic even though his concern is now about the social condition of mankind. His concern has widened to include mankind, but the "hell is other people" quality of Sartrean thought remains. In painting the big picture, he still allows the other person to be blurred over, as it were. Even for Sartre the Marxist and man of acute social conscience, it seems that one is committed to oneself.

PERMANENCE AND COMMUNION

The importance given to freedom in the thought of Jean Paul Sartre is given to communion in the philosophy of Gabriel Marcel. This contemporary of Sartre's, who

[6] Jean Paul Sartre, *Critique de la Raison Dialectique* (Paris: Gallimard, 1960).

was also an existentialist philosopher, was fond of pointing out that all of his philosophical reflections were one long meditation on the meaning of "with." He concentrates on the area of the intersubjective: *co-être* rather than *être* if you will. In contrast to Sartre's "hell is other people," Marcel is convinced that "there is only one suffering, to be alone."

Marcel explores all those human experiences that border on the religious, such as the experiences of love and hope and fidelity. His optic is always the intersubjective. He sees the aspiration for human communion underneath all human striving. In communion the human spirit flourishes; outside of it, it wilts. One could say that communion is each person's fundamental project, if one wanted to be Marcelean in his thought and Sartrean in his language.

In my own terms, communion flows naturally from indwelling, just as indwelling flows from self-donation. Like indwelling, communion is created and sustained by words and deeds. The deeds that bring it about and keep it in existence are many—generically, the deeds of caring and sharing, giving and receiving. Deeds done in love generate communion. But words, too, create, sustain (or ruin) communion. The words that create and sustain communion are many. But chief among them are words of love which carry promises with them, and chief among these, of course, is the promise of "forever."

Human communion naturally involves more than two people. The child who is the fruit of the union of a man and a woman is the most obvious symbol of this extension. But communion grows beyond the family; it embraces a whole network of relationships, each reinforcing the other. Ideally, a communion will have a relationship of indwelling at the heart of it, but it is not to be judged inauthentic if it does not.

The religious person will be conscious of how large a part God plays in the creation of human communion. The deeply religious person will believe that God is the Omega to which all human communion tends as well as the power that brings it into existence. The knowledgeable Christian will see in human communion the raw material, at least, if not the reality, of the kingdom of God. Communion is the natural milieu of the person, the milieu in which the person grows. Outside of it, person growth does not take place. Anything, therefore, that would jeopardize the communion that has already been constituted imperils the growth and well-being of persons.

Human communion is broken by the absence of love, by breaking promises, by withdrawing one's word, by changing the meaning of one's word, by infidelity. But Marcel puts his finger on something more subtle than any of these, which is also inimical to human communion. He develops the helpful distinction that shows two different ways of living-out one's lifelong commitments. He observes that some perseverance in commitments takes place at a superficial level inasmuch as some people live in a way that has them do what they said they would do, and they do it dutifully. If they merit praise for having fulfilled the terms of the promises they made, they win no plaudits from Marcel. He calls this kind of perseverance "constancy." But mere constancy can have a demeaning effect on the one for whom one fulfills one's duties. Fidelity, on the other hand, is more than the performance of promised actions. It is constancy plus unction of heart. By fidelity, according to Marcel's use of the term, one preserves the interior sentiments that initially caused the person to commit himself. When the love which inspired the initial promise continues to animate the one promising and the one to whom the promise has been made, then neither party will become an object of the other's duty.

Marcel's distinction is a good reminder of how wrong it is to look at our own lives or the lives of others merely in terms of behavior, because according to that measure, constancy and fidelity would be undifferentiated. Marcel's distinction is also a good reminder that it is not the intention of permanence that should keep a commitment intact. A union of hearts is the stuff of human commitment. If such a union exists, many difficulties can be withstood. If a union of hearts is slight or virtually nonexistent, then any difficulty can bring the fragile relationship to an end. To aim at permanence in commitment is sterile. To aim at a greater union of hearts within the communion already experienced will be a more effective and efficacious way of attaining permanence in commitment. Concentration on permanence looks at an effect rather than a cause. "Permanent" is an after-the-fact description of a commitment that has been true to the communion within which it operated.

I find this category of communion a much more helpful criterion for discerning commitment questions than the category of freedom which can be too individualistically conceived of. Communion is not so conceptually objectifiable that one is tempted to deal with the mystery of commitment that takes place within it as if either were univocal realities. The category of communion, like the reality of communion, approaches commitment questions

78

from a "we are" perspective rather than a Sartrean one, which I think is too solitary. One can appreciate the fact that every communion, every "we are," is as unique as every "I."

Is there any justification for withdrawing from a permanent commitment? The answer must be sought in terms of communion. It must be dealt with in terms of oneself and others. In general, one could say that withdrawal from a permanent commitment is as undersirable as the removal of a plant from the earth which nourishes it. But, to continue the image, if the plant is dying in the soil in which it has been embedded or if it has never grown in that soil, then that's another matter. Transplants are called for at times. In other words, when the communion which the commitment should have led to, or to which it aspired, is nonexistent and gives no sign of being able to come into existence, then withdrawal from one's permanent commitment may be warranted.

But an immediate *caveat* suggests itself. The claim that communion does not exist or that it cannot exist in a given case will be much more frequent than the fact that it does not or cannot exist. What may look and feel like incompatibility between persons or between a person and a state of life is often simple resistance to the pain that growth requires. Unable to distinguish the pain of growth from incompatibility, the person is just as likely to be discontent in the next would-be permanent relationship as he or she was in the first one.

The fact is that the person or persons with whom we

are most immediately linked are not only the source of our growth, they are also the immediate causes of the "dying" that is necessary for our growth. They stand at the intimate paschal juncture where we continually pass over from self-absorption into self-donation and communion. Sometimes the point at which fuller life is attained will seem more like death than at other times. An individual who refuses to accept the paschal nature of love (i.e., dying and rising) frequently conjures up in his imagination prospective relationships and situations in which only one half of the reality of love and commitment are operating. That is, the enthusiastic, all-high, exhilarating side of it. One can easily move from that mistake to imagining living in communion with still unborn or untested relationships which escape routine and produce ongoing highs. Since this condition of life is not possible and not real, more than one person will be used to try to attain it. A musical-chairs mentality develops if a person refuses to see that indwelling and communion come about by dealing with and working through misunderstandings, boredom, mutual hardships, lack of communication, character deficiencies, each other's sinfulness, and the natural sufferings that flesh is heir to. Human relationships, human communion, require an acceptance of darkness with light, the pedestrian with the exhilarating. Once transcendence is sought by trying to circumvent the limitations of the particular, communion will never be achieved.

Can obligation hold a commitment together? It obviously can, but should it? To relate to another in terms of obligation might be all right for justice interactions, but it is not the stuff that makes for human communion. A period of obligation can be endured in interpersonal commitments if it shows promise of leading to human communion. The obligatory can flower into love. But it can also ruin forever the possibility of any degree of communion if it demeans the recipient by making commitment to him an object of duty, not to mention how impoverishing it is for the actor. At the same time, I doubt there is any human, interpersonal love totally devoid of actions undertaken out of a sense of obligation. Some of this is inevitable; much of this is dangerous.

I would like to be more specific here about some of these points, but the further one descends into particulars about commitment the more complex and unique the matter becomes. The following remarks are meant, therefore, to be merely concrete observations which may or may not enlighten the commitment situations the reader has in mind. They do not pretend to be thorough treatments of the areas raised.

It is a common experience of many marriages that the actual commitment of oneself to another is made long after the words of permanent commitment are spoken. Not that the initial "I do" when pronounced is insincere, but the full "yes" frequently does not come until the person is capable of a more total choice. This *later* moment presumes that greater maturity and freedom and self-knowledge have taken place in the interim, but even more, it presumes a highly developed knowledge of the other which was not there at first. The point is that many marriages that have gone through many years in great difficulty end up successfully. A more perfect communion can be achieved later. Because the parties were "faithful over a few things," they were able to enter into a hitherto unexperienced joy in a commitment that finally came to fruition, sometimes years after it was made.

In this connection, we could profitably ponder the subject of hope in relation to commitment. Every commitment is a human act of hope (not to mention faith and love as well). All interpersonal commitments, like faith itself, must be lived more in hope than in the full experience of communion. Perfect communion takes place when the indwelling is one of complete love, love so unadulterated that more than two indwell the reality of it. (This is why in heaven "there will be no marrying or giving in marriage.") The less perfect communions we live in, here in time, will be of a "first fruits" sort. By that, I mean that in varying degrees there will be a tangible experience of communion, but never so complete that one can repose in it. Enough of an experience to confirm the process of self-donation that brings it about; enough to make one want more; enough to know that there will be a continuity between the present communion and what is to come in full measure in the future; enough to live in hope. In some instances, like the one cited above, the parties will live for years much more conscious of their hope for a communion that is not yet experienced than in hope within an experienced communion.

What is suspect in the area of marriage is the claim of incompatibility after mutual compatibility, i.e., some degree of indwelling and, in turn, communion has been experienced. The initial experience proves that all the ingredients of success were there at one time and makes it much more likely that something that can be surmounted has entered in to weaken the marriage bond. The fact that some degree of indwelling was once enjoyed suggests the possibility that it can be achieved anew if worked at and the needed correctives are introduced. (The presence of children would seem to be further reminders that what had once been achieved can be reachieved.)

Some permanent commitments are taken in a community, such as religious-life communities in the Roman Catholic Church. What justification is there for withdrawing from such a community in which one has permanently committed oneself? The answer again relates to the presence or absence of communion. But the reason why communion has not taken place must be asked of both the individual who withdraws his or her commitment and of the community itself. The inviolate nature of each person's commitments, as inviolate as his conscience, must be respected at this point. Nevertheless, some questions are appropriate. What reason does the individual have for thinking that the absence of communion he experiences is the fault of the community rather than himself? The community, after all, is made up of a number of individuals, and if the individual in question has not been able to attain to some degree of communion when a large number of people are accessible to him, what is solved by withdrawal from the community?

There are questions to be asked of the community also. If a number of people withdraw from a community in which they have permanently committed themselves, obviously the quality of the relationships within that community must be scrutinized. A large number of withdrawals indicates that a need is not being met, a union of hearts is not being achieved. If some degree of communion with others within which the process of self-donation can take place is not being achieved with members of the

SHOULD ANYONE SAY FOREVER?

community, is there enough space being allowed by the community for such communion to take place within a wider circle, with individuals who are not a part of the community?

One of the main reasons for noncommunion in religious life is that frequently adolescent patterns of communication and relationship develop early and are never tempered or matured by outside influences. One of the best ways to overcome this deficiency is for the community to give the individual enough space for this to take place. Obviously, it would be ideal if the most important persons in one's life were also members of one's own community. But there was no guarantee when one took one's vows that this would be the case. Desirable as that might be, there is no way of predetermining this over the course of a life. Perpetual vows in a community mean, among other things, the promise of one's presence to and with and in that community. But one cannot promise that all his or her becoming will take place within the matrix of relationships of the community itself. What one can and must promise, if religious life is to mean anything, is that one's becoming will be shared with the community. It is not enough to integrate one's radical loves, whether these are with members of one's religious community or outside it, with one's commitment to God. One must also integrate these in the flesh-and-blood life of the community to which one has given oneself. One's willingness, even need, to do this will be a good sign of the pedigree of the relationships one has and a good measure of the depths of communion one seeks with his or her community.

These are difficult things to reduce to clarities. It seems, however, that there are two kinds of extremists in the relationship between an individual and the community to which he has committed himself. There are the centrifugalists and the centripetalists. The centrifugalists (those who flee, and move away from the center) act as if their community is a means to ends which they themselves determine. The community must serve their needs so that they can serve others, the centrifugalists would say. The community is the base from which they operate, the center from which they go forth to do their work. Obviously, such an attitude can easily mask the heart of a cad or become illusory. As in a trial marriage, the individual can begin to see himself standing over against the community, which he constantly judges for its ability to satisfy him. While he puts the community in a difficult, if not impossible, position, he himself is in a no-loss position. He easily becomes the taker rather than the giver, the one who calculates rather than gives of himself, the one who observes rather than participates. Self-absorption rather than self-donation is almost inevitable in this extreme. (We might also note in passing that this is a new wrinkle in religious life. It used to be that religious communities were prone to treat individuals as if they were means to accomplish the ends which the community set for itself. Now the opposite is frequently the case, where the community is the means and the individual determines the ends he will pursue.) This extreme is more frequent among male religious than female. His commitment easily becomes specialized tasks, and self-donation does not take place because the person has put the highest priority on achieving the tasks which he considers worth his life.

The centripetalists are at the opposite extreme. They seek community avidly. This extreme (and remember, it is the extreme only that I am trying to describe) is more prevalent among women than among men. Just as the centrifugalists come close to having an exploitative attitude toward the community, so the centripetalists turn the community into a source of security, a nest into which they can settle. Behind their talk about the need for greater community or their seeming dedication to the community, one can find flight from, and refusal to be stretched by, life and the risks of loving. Settling in becomes an overriding concern. Once becoming no longer takes place, self-donation is impossible and communion is out of the question. Communities comprised of settlers (as opposed to seekers) are innocent of the experience of communion.

In this chapter we have attempted to analyze the property of permanence that attaches to some of our commitments. We have inquired into some of the sources of the modern uncertainty about this property. Permanence has not been found to be alien to love relationships but internal to them. Personal growth and the intention of permanence have also been found to be intrinsically linked. The most effective way human beings have of expressing the quality of totality in their commitment relationships with one another is to have recourse to quantity, indicating that one's commitment is not limited to a given time but holds forever. Permanent commitment has no justification if its object is impersonal or if in either its inspiration or its intention it is lacking in love. Finally, we sought to contrast the individualism of Sartre's fundamental project with Gabriel Marcel's category of communion in order to begin to develop a criterion for judging the particular questions that permanent commitments pose.

Chapter IV
Two Axial Commitments

The subject of commitment can be explored by proceeding from ideas to reality, or it can proceed from actual instances of commitment to the construction of a theological understanding about it. In this portion of our study we will proceed in the latter way, beginning with actual commitments made, in the hope that we can derive from them more about the characteristics that seem proper to such an act and condition of being.

So much for how to begin. Where to begin—or to be more precise, with whom?—is another question. All things being equal, the more totally committed the persons studied, the more light they are likely to shed on what a commitment is or isn't. It seems to me that the two most complete commitments ever made that Christians have access to were those of Jesus of Nazareth to Yahweh and the commitment of God the Father to his only Son. On them all of reality reposes. Through these two commitments, all of creation and, in turn, the new creation come into being. Although neither of these commitments can be plumbed to its depths, even a brief and superficial examination of them should prove to be a worthwhile exercise. Any intelligibility we believe we have arrived at so far on this subject should be submitted to, and judged by, the light which comes from these two commitments. And any subsequent insight should be integrated into, and made consonant with, what we come to see in these two axial commitments. Since they are at the core of the reality we know and live in, they should serve to test any prior, and to ground any further, notions about commitment that we glean from other sources.

An objection can be raised immediately against such an approach. If our study thus far has focused on interpersonal commitments, how can the theological and religious data that comes from Scripture and the Christian tradition serve to illumine our question? It would seem that these sources will be irrelevant, the objection could run, since they deal with man's relation to God and God's relation to man.

This objection requires that I indicate some of the presuppositions I take to such a question. First of all, I believe that one's relationship with God affects one's comportment with his children. Even a small amount of faith affects one's behavior. The more one believes in God, the more faith will shape one's life and therefore one's commitments. Furthermore, since most of my understanding of commitment has come from my observation and experience of believing Christians (as well as from my own understanding, and attempt, to live Christianly), it is only natural that the frame of reference I use in analyzing interpersonal commitment is one in which the Christian faith plays a major role. It therefore warrants explicit treatment.

But more importantly, I believe that the Scriptures are as much a statement about human beings as they are about God: men and women, that is, as God sees them. Consequently, the light of revelation illumines the world of human relationships much more profoundly than reason alone or unaided reflection on experience could do. In the light of God's word we are given to see what could be and ought to be our relations with one another. Hence the power of revelation to further our understanding into the mystery of commitment. Besides, I have found the Scriptures to be the best literature available on the subject matter of our study, so I have no desire to apologize for having recourse to them.

Furthermore, God is personal and a person to those who believe in him. So if one is committed to him, one's commitment is interpersonal. Admittedly, God is a person in a way that is only analogous to human persons, and one's commitment to him is, of course, only analogous to one's commitment to another, but there is a mutuality here.

If we have any doubts that a person's commitment to God can and should be interpersonal and that this commitment affects our relationship with our fellow human beings, we might reflect on the fact that the ideal for human behavior which Jesus taught was: "You must be perfect even as your heavenly Father is perfect" (Matt. 5:48). This suggests that God's own behavior toward us— that is to say, our perception of him and his way of relating to us—is meant to be the ideal against which we project our behavior toward one another.

I believe, finally, that the subject of commitment cannot be dealt with satisfactorily outside of a religious context or frame of reference. Not only do I think it cannot be understood in a satisfactory way outside of such a context, I do not think it ultimately makes sense outside of such a frame of reference. So much for the objection and the presuppositions we bring to the material that follows.

THE COMMITMENT OF THE FATHER TO THE SON

Although we probably never thought of it quite this way before, it would be fruitful to consider the relationship of the Father to his eternal Son in terms of a commitment. If this were merely an invitation to speculate on the intratrinitarian life, we could not hope to derive much understanding from such an exercise. But since "the immanent Trinity is the economic Trinity," as Karl Rahner has so ably demonstrated, we are not left dataless about the inner life of the Godhead. That is to say, the eternal mystery of the relation of the Father to his only Son comes within the range of human perception in the incarnation. We can start with this more accessible moment in their eternal relationship and work backward and forward from that point in time.

The conferral of human life on Jesus was a gift from God, the author of life. The conception and birth of every human being is as much. But with Jesus there was a more immediate, a more intimate nexus between the gift-nature of the life he received and God who gave it. "The Holy Spirit will come upon you, and the power of the most high will overshadow you," Mary was informed when she inquired as to the manner of Jesus' birth. "And so the child will be holy and will be called Son of God" (Luke 1:34-35).

The content, so to speak, of the Father's commitment to his Son was more than human life; it was the Father's own mode of existence. Jesus lived *because* of his Father in a way no other human son does with respect to his human father. In the latter instance, the father ceases to be necessary for the son's existence after the moment of conception. But God's Son is "explained" neither in time nor in eternity by anything less than his own Father's eternal union with him and the irrevocable gift of existence to his Son. The Father's act of self-donation is as eternal as God himself, since there never was a time when the Son "was not."

We cannot proceed further in understanding the Father's commitment to his Son without mentioning the relationship of both to the Spirit. In the theological tradition, the Spirit came to be called Love. In addition, the Spirit was seen as the bond of love between Father and Son as well as the fruit of the love of Father and Son. All three descriptions add some degree of intelligibility to the commitment relationship between Father and Son. The Father can confer the fullness of divine being on his Son and yet remain distinct, not only because of the incommunicability of his paternity but because the love he has for his Son both binds him to his Son and is itself subsistent being that is Spirit. Systematic theology would go on to describe this intratrinitarian reality as comprised of irreducible relations of opposition. Without getting that far into the speculative part of trinitarian theology, we can see something of this suggested in the more tangible Gospel data, which appreciates the fact that for Jesus the

91

ever-present evidence of his Father's love for him was the Spirit. The Father's way of being faithful to Jesus was to confer upon him his own abiding Spirit. And, of course, Jesus' way of being a loving and faithful Son of his Father was by his continual attention to the presence and promptings of the abiding Spirit. The Spirit made it possible for the Son to indwell the divine reality and vice versa. The Spirit gift makes indwelling possible and communion inevitable. The perfection of communion and indwelling is the Trinity.

There are many adumbrations of the content of the Father's commitment to his Son in the Old Testament. In some ways the commitment factor in their relationship is more recognizable in these more ancient disclosures than it is in the New Testament. Take, for example, the description of the Godhead contained in the prophet Daniel's vision:

> As Daniel watched, thrones were set up and the Ancient One took his throne. His clothing was snow white and the hair on his head was white as wool. His throne was flame of fire with wheels of burning fire. A surging stream of fire flowed out from where he sat. Thousands upon thousands were administering to him, and myriads upon myriads attended him. The court was convened and the books were opened. As the visions during the night continued, I saw one like to a Son of Man coming on the clouds of heaven. When he reached the Ancient One and was presented before him, He received dominion, glory and kingship. Nations and people of every language served him. His dominion is an everlasting dominion that should not be taken away, his kingship shall not be destroyed (Dan 7:9–14).

The Christian will see more here, of course, than the Old Testament author saw or intended to communicate. Fire will become a symbol of the presence of the Spirit. The Son of Man will become the favorite title of Jesus of Nazareth. And the Ancient One will be seen as Father by those who believe in Jesus. But what is central to the passage and germane to our study is the remarkable commitment the Ancient One is making to the Son of Man. The Son of Man receives "dominion, glory and kingship," the very things that constitute the Ancient One's own kingship. The unconditional conferral of this power on the mysterious figure called the Son of Man, evidently without prior warning or cause, elevates him to the status of royalty. He exercises the kind of power and dominion which was previously reserved to the Ancient One alone. Although this scene is rudimentary as far as the revelation of the Trinity is concerned, it does disclose something of the commitment the Ancient One makes to the Son of Man. When the trinitarian revelation becomes fuller—in the Christian economy, in other words—the depths of that commitment will be visible for the first time. Then it will be seen that the so-called Ancient One did not bestow something on someone, but the fullness of divine life and love on his own Son.

Self-donation, in brief, is the essence of the Father's commitment to his Son. Later theology will speculate about the mutual relations within the Trinity and see the entire personalities of each of the divine persons constituted by their complete self-donation to one another. Each divine person is uniquely himself by reason of his self-donation to the other two divine persons. In other words, complete commitment to the other in love is at the heart and core of the internal life of God himself.

The Father's commitment to his Son, furthermore, included the unconditional intention that all subsequent existents were to come into being through his Son. All of creation was to be shaped by his own Son's purposes, subject to his dominion, and destined finally for his glory. Anthropomorphically speaking, we might say that the entire future of the universe was shaped by the Father's act of self-donation. It is as if the Father were saying: "Henceforth and forever I will make no choices absolutely or by reason of my sovereignty. My Son will shape the *not yet*, and the created reality which He shapes will be forever filial in my eyes." The Father's commitment specifies how the future will be configured without at the same time predetermining it. This is an act of trust of staggering proportions, for in a sense the Father is entrusting himself to his Son. If, according to Jesus, "the Father and I are one," then "the Son and I are one," the Father says. The Father places not only the *not yet* of the universe in the hands of his Son, but in a manner of speaking he places the *not yet* of his own person in his Son's hands. The aphorism that the Son would one day teach his followers that "he who loses his life shall find it" applied also to his Father. It is precisely because of his self-gift to his Son that he becomes Father.

Just as we used the Daniel text to look back from the moment of the incarnation into the pre-existence of Jesus, so now we will look forward to the resurrection in an attempt to understand more fully the commitment of the Father to Jesus. We can fruitfully look on the whole of Jesus' earthly life as an exemplification of the Father's

94

commitment to his only Son. But the paramount event that exemplifies this commitment is the resurrection. At that moment Jesus, "in the order of the Spirit, the Spirit of holiness that was in him, was proclaimed Son of God in all His power through his resurrection from the dead" (Rom. 1:4). By raising him from the dead, the Father showed at this moment most precisely the nature of his eternal commitment to his only Son. Jesus was raised because he was one with God's own life, which is eternal. From all eternity the Father had committed himself to relating to his Son as the unbegotten to the begotten. Jesus was this begotten Son and, though he was made flesh, his Father would not allow him to undergo corruption and decay. As a result of his exultation, his being raised to the Father's right hand, Jesus receives the name "that is above all names" because it is proper to God alone. Jesus is called Lord, with the result that "at the name of Jesus all beings in the heaven and on earth and in the underworld should bend the knee, and every tongue should acclaim Jesus Christ as Lord to the glory of God the Father" (Phil. 2:11). That which was true from all eternity became perceivable to us in time.

Nothing we have learned in the previous part of our study is contradicted by what we have seen here. In fact, the opposite is true. What we learned in the initial part is complemented by what we see here. Several things, therefore, can be concluded about the commitment of the Father to his only Son which throw more light on the meaning of commitment. First of all, we can see that this commitment touches more than the order of the Father's intention. It affects the order of existence itself. Insofar as the Son is the term of the Father's commitment, this statement should be obvious. But more than that, this commitment also affects the Father's mode of existence. It is not simply an act of the will that goes out from the person of the Father, it is also, so to speak, an act whereby the person of the Father goes out from himself and gains therein the completion of his own selfhood. Without this commitment of himself the Father would not be Father, since he would not have a Son. He would be still the Ancient One, or Yahweh, Elohim, El Shaddai, or Lord, but not Father. His commitment, therefore, completes his personhood. One would have to conclude that, at least in the case of God, commitment is not a take-it-or-leave-it component of his inner life but is at the center of it. Since we are made in his image and likeness, could it be any less so for us?

Secondly, this commitment affects more than the Father and the Son. It is generative of existence beyond itself. The act that anteceded the creation of the universe, the act through which all that is came to be, was an act of commitment. Human commitments also affect the order of existence in their own way, perfecting it, realigning it, adding to it, deepening it (and in some cases perverting it). Every interpersonal commitment has a generative affect beyond itself. Every interpersonal commitment can create a communion, or it can weaken, even destroy, the communion that is already there.

Thirdly, the Father's commitment to his Son is further indication of what we have already seen, that freedom and commitment are not of themselves incompatible. Certainly, the specification that this act of love entailed has not been confining. The love which generated this commitment still diffuses itself through the Son into the ongoing creation of a universe. The variety, immensity, and richness of created reality should be constant witnesses to the fact that neither the Father nor the Son are confined by the Father's commitment of himself to the Son (or the Son's commitment to the Father).

All of creation as well as the universal redemption come through the particularization of the Father's love in the Son and in the word made flesh. Because of the eternal generation of the Son we were made, and because of the incarnation all will be made anew. Because the Father in a sense entrusted himself to his Son, we will be freed from our sins. Ultimately, it was because of the Father's self-donation and self-entrustment to his only Son that our creation and redemption came to be. We should be able to see from this, if from nothing else, that seeking fullness and transcendence by trying to avoid particularizing our capacity to give ourselves in love is misguided.

JESUS' COMMITMENT

The purpose of this portion of the study will be to focus on the life of Jesus as a life of commitment. In him we can see more deeply into the mystery of human commitment, I believe, than we can through any other interpersonal commitment ever made. We will begin with a few of the things that leap out immediately from reflection on his life in terms of commitment:

* He was accused by no one of being undercommitted; he was accused by many of being overcommitted.
* The object of his commitment was unmistakable: Yahweh, whom he perceived as his Father; about him, Jesus was unreserved in his obedience, trust and praise.

97

* His commitment to his Father was interpersonal without, however, being egalitarian.
* Jesus' commitment to his Father cannot be adequately distinguished from his love of his Father.
* The effect of his commitment was that it gave his life its direction; and because of it he was free.
* His commitment was total from the beginning but always new in the ways it was shown.
* The seemingly religious commitments of other Israelites constituted the greatest obstacle he had in being heard; the least religiously committed were the most ready to listen to him.
* His commitment did not make him myopic or brittle or aprioristic; his enemies, on the other hand, seemed to be all of these.
* His commitment to his Father did not exclude; rather, it enhanced his capacity for communion with others.

But after these more evident ideas impress themselves on you, a number of questions pose themselves. I wonder if Jesus was conscious of being committed? Certainly the kind of love he had casts out the form of voluntarism that undertakes actions out of a sense of obligation. But when love is as perfect as his was for his Father, does commitment frame one's consciousness or does it fall away in favor of more other-regarding dynamics?

Was his love of his Father the only "form" his commitment needed? Or is that too disembodied for a human being? In this connection, Israel and the law come up. Was Jesus committed to Israel?

How did his commitment to God connect itself with his obedience to the law?

How did his commitment to God affect his capacity to
commit himself in love to others?

Was Jesus free to make a less total commitment to his Father than the one he made? Would our redemption
have been won if he did?

We will deal with some of these questions and insights
more fully in what follows, but before proceeding, one
preliminary note should be made. Christians have definite
Christologies, though these are usually more implicit than
explicit. One's Christology will determine whether commitment in the life of Jesus is a real or an unreal question.
If a person has embraced an ascending Christology—that
is, one in which Jesus' sameness with the rest of us, his
humanness in other words, is emphasized—then Jesus'
commitment will be seen as important. If our Christology,
on the other hand, tends to be a descending one—that is,
one that emphasizes his divinity and his pre-existence as
Son of God—the question of his commitment will seem
less important because one will have the image of Jesus as
always acting from the center of his divinity. His divine
nature is so in charge, in this image of him, that his
human behavior will seem to flow inexorably from this
inner divinity. His human decisions and struggles then
will seem to be relatively minor features of his personality, since they will be caught up and swept along in the
rush from the inner ontological unity he enjoyed with the
Godhead. The definite bias of what follows will be the
former one of an ascending Christology.

The Gospels make it obvious that Jesus' commitment
was to his Father. What they make less evident is the development that took place within him concerning his commitment. The commitment of the child was different from

the commitment of the adolescent, and so on. If one is human, one becomes. Being human, Jesus became with respect to his commitment. He did not enjoy from the beginning a complete vision of what his commitment to his Father would entail, nor its relationship to the Israel within which his commitment was made. He would not have known at first either the price or the prize his commitment was to bring him. The light he had at any one stage about what was being asked of him came from his prayer, his experiences, his sufferings, his teachers, and his own continual sifting of the traditions that held together the religious and social context of Jewish society. "During his life on earth he offered prayer and entreaty, aloud and in silent tears . . . although he was Son, he learned to obey through suffering" (Heb. 5:7–9). There was nothing of the automatic about this process. The abiding tutor of the process which continually brought him out of darkness into sufficient light to discern the particular objects and immediate direction he was to take was the Spirit.

It is apparent on every page of the Gospels that Jesus' commitment is never less than total, while at the same time it is always in process. This does not mean that it is partial or conditional or imperfect. The child Jesus was not being remiss about his Father's business because he failed to take whip in hand and flail the money-changers in his first visit to the temple.

All living is a process of becoming. In the course of the process, one must face the risk of loving. Loving is a choice one makes to share his becoming with another or others. One way of looking at Jesus' commitment is to see it as his ongoing choice that his becoming take place with the Other, who was revealing himself to him as Father.

His life shows this intentionality. In every aspect we can see his becoming take place with his Father. Consciousness of his Father is evident in all the particulars of his life, even those as innocuous as the flight of birds or the color of flowers or the fecundity of fig trees. The way he approached people left no doubt in their minds about the transcendent object of his commitment and source of his love. He never acted or spoke as if he were alone. The unself-conscious way he spoke about his Father and his penchant for spending whole nights alone in prayer, as well as the degree of upset he experienced when the things of his Father, such as his "Father's house," were perverted, all indicate the *ad Patrem* direction of his life, the depth of his commitment, and the degree to which he shared his becoming with him. He did not make decisions as one who was alone; he did not speak as one who considered his wisdom self-generated; he did not act as a solitary but as one who chose the yoke of love as his way of becoming.

People did not find him bogged down with intellectual or legal or theological baggage when they approached him. His wisdom always seemed to come forth unrehearsed and fresh and from a deeper perspective on the moment than others could enunciate. His responses to persons and his reactions to situations show a man who is fully present to both while his primordial commitment to his Father is never in question or remote. The need of his enemies to scheme constantly to deflect the unidirectional intentionality of his whole being should be taken as proof of the fullness of Jesus' commitment.

In one sense, becoming is inevitable. There is no way of holding back its inexorable onrush. In another sense, we are free to resist becoming. Those contemporaries of Jesus who resisted becoming and opted for an opposite kind of life than Jesus' shielded themselves against life and becoming with their a priori's. They handled life by categorizing behavior, especially that of others. The only spontaneity they showed was when they vented their spleen at someone like Jesus who refused to live and act and speak within their brittle categories. The preservation of their categories became an obsession with them. People and people's needs took second place to their preservation. For all practical purposes, what they wanted Jesus to do was leave them alone. "Don't, therefore, heal the shriveled limb on the Sabbath." "Don't disturb our property so that your hungry might eat." "Don't stir up demons if it means we will lose our swine." "Don't confuse us by teaching us new things about God and ourselves." "We have the law and it will take care of us, thank you." They had twisted the law into something that served them. It re-enforced their self-absorption and impeded their self-donation.

In the indwelling that transpired between Jesus and his Father we can see the perfect interrelationship between love and commitment. They do not necessarily go together. One's commitments can be motivated by things other than love, and legitimately so. Self-improvement, the need to achieve, economic solvency, a desire for meaningful activity, justice, a need for companionship, a desire to be of service to others—these and many other motivations can impel one to make and keep commitments, even heroic ones. By the same token, who is unaware of instances when love does not flower, for whatever reasons, into a commitment to the other? What is ideal for interpersonal commitments is when the motivating force that has made and kept them is love. A commitment motivated by love should both express and insure the condition of being we have called indwelling.

Indwelling reveals itself in everything Jesus does and in the way he thinks and speaks about himself. It is not his commitment as such that impels him, but the love he has for his Father. Though distinguishable, love and commitment were never separated in Jesus. This was not inevitable. It is conceivable that his commitment could have been made initially out of love of his Father but not sustained from that center. As it does in so many other relationships, his commitment could have lost its nexus with the love that brought it into being and become something to be persevered in for its own sake or for some motive other than love.

Though Jesus' commitment to his Father was total, it is quite evident from the Gospels that this did not mean that it was disincarnate or that it was impossible for him to make a commitment in love to anyone else. In other words, Jesus' life shows the connection not only between love and commitment but also between indwelling and communion. If anything, the intensity of his commitment to his Father created a greater capacity to love and commit himself to others. The fact that his Father came first did not impede him from loving others, even to the point of laying down his life for his friends. His love of others was of a piece with, in harmony with, and proof of his love for his Father. There were many different degrees in these relationships. He was committed to those he taught, but not to the same degree as to those whom he invited to walk with him. And even among his followers there were those for whom he clearly showed a preference; some he brought closer than others. This was also true of those whom he regarded as his friends, such as Mary and Martha and their brother Lazarus.

It would be perplexing to read John's teaching (I John 4:12) that we must show our love for the God whom we don't see by our love of our brothers whom we see, if this were not also true of Jesus. A distorted notion of Jesus' love of his Father has been used too often to justify a disincarnate kind of Christianity, one in which, in the name of the love of God, a person gives his love and commits himself to no one. This spiritualization of commitment, the attempt to concoct a paradigm that is fleshless and without anything to symbolize it, is rooted in fantasy and repugnant to the realism of the Gospel. The most sacred of vows professing complete love of God has often concealed the concomitant intention of withholding oneself from others, remaining aloof from the risk, the pain, and the joy of commitment to human beings.

Jesus felt that this ruse was being perpetrated by many of his contemporaries. In the name of commitment, they were perverting the religious and human meaning of commitment. Recall, for example, the way he castigated some of the Pharisees for their treatment of their own parents. They would claim that the goods they owned had been dedicated to God (in the rite called "corban"), and, in a manner of speaking, they were. This meant that they could not be put at the disposal of people, their parents in particular, no matter how needy they were. They would then hypocritically lament to their parents: "Anything I have that I might have used to help you is dedicated to God," and be rid of their duty to father or mother (Matt. 15:4–7). A commitment to God that cost them nothing was the justification they used to avoid a commitment to another that would cost something.

The faithful and the faithless lived side by side in the Israel of Jesus' day. Both professed their belief in and love of and commitment to Yahweh. The principal way by which Jesus discerned the difference between the authentic and the phony in the matter of commitment to God was the way people dealt with one another. The widespread practice of remaining aloof from the needs of another and insisting that others remain aloof in the name of a higher commitment was vehemently denounced by him. When people were dealt with as mere occasions for observing the law, when they were fitted into the confines of the letter of the law, when they were made means to one's growth in righteousness, Jesus knew how perverted commitment had become in much of Israel. Sins of omission were one thing, but in the name of commitment to Yahweh, heavy burdens were continually being laid on the shoulders of the meek and the poor. We can almost hear his exasperation: "It's one thing to neglect and turn away from the whole process of self-donation; it's another to place impossible obstacles in the way of persons who are prepared to go that route." In the name of commitment the majority of Israel's leaders pursued a life of self-absorption (or unloving righteousness) and did their best to see that the rest of the people followed in their tracks.

The consequences to mankind of Jesus' commitment are too many to narrate. Let us consider, therefore, the effects of his commitment on Jesus himself. The Gospels give us a fascinating picture of a man of undeviating purpose who, at the same time, is always hanging loose. If he had been simply one or the other, he would have come across as a fanatic or a hobo. Instead, he began to resemble the characteristics of the one he loved and spoke so familiarly about. He is a perfect example of the truism: "You become what you love." He becomes like the one to whom he had committed himself in love. He becomes an exemplary instance of the beautiful things he says about his Father. Like Father, like Son.

Neither his words nor his deeds, as the Gospels record them, show any irresolution or confusion, so complete is the integration of his life around his Father. Because his own sense of direction was so undeviating, he felt keenly the aimlessness of the people, seeing them as meandering, directionless, shepherdless sheep. The invitation he issued to follow him came because, by comparison, he was certain about where he had come from and where he was going. He paid dearly for extending such an invitation. If his commitment to his Father had not included those who were wandering around aimlessly before they walked with him, he probably would have only suffered the ostracism of the authorities. If he had kept his commitment tidily transcendent and uninvolved with people, he would not have met with a violent death.

His whole life is one long commentary on St. Paul's observation: "Where the Spirit is, there is freedom" (II Cor. 3:18). His commitment did not bind him, it freed him. It freed him from aimlessness, meaninglessness, confinement in his own solitude. It freed him from having to see himself and accept himself in the terms in which others insisted on seeing him. It freed him from the tyranny of others' whim and fancy, judgment and suspicion, adulation and rejection. He was free from having to act on the basis of fear of others, even the most paralyzing fear that men can hold over other men: fear of death at their hands. He was not without fear; if he had been, he wouldn't have been one of us. But even his fear of death at the hands of men was caught up and integrated into the powerful vortex of his trust and commitment to his Father. Note his teaching in this regard: "Do not be afraid of those who can kill the body and after that can do no more. I will tell you whom to fear: fear him who, after he has killed, has the power to cast into hell. Yes, I tell you, fear him" (Luke 12:4–5).

His commitment did not bind him, it loosed him. A commitment serves the function of a yoke. Ironically, there is no human freedom outside of a yoke. There is no way of living fully without loving, and there is no love that is not a yoke, which is to say a complementarity that leads to life. The trick is not to try to avoid the yoke but to submit to it freely and in love. Depending on what one determines to be yoked to—or to whom, I should say— one will be either free or bound. We know what the effect was on Jesus' law-yoked contemporaries. They became legalistic and racked by their mania for righteousness. Jesus, on the other hand, takes on the qualities of the one to whom he gave himself. It should not be surprising, therefore, that in the Gospels he begins to manifest a freedom from the limitations of matter. Even before his death and resurrection we see him showing a connaturality for such unusual actions as walking over wind-swept water. He becomes like the one he loves, and the one he loves is Lord of the winds and the waves, life and death, victory and defeat. The more complete his commitment to his Father, the more like his Father he became.

It would be fruitful to investigate a little further the

kind of freedom Jesus' commitment brought him. It was not the freedom of indetermination but the freedom that truth brings with it. Not the truth associated with abstractions or propositions or systems, but the truth that Jesus learned, under the tutelage of the Spirit, about himself. This was the truth that made him free. It was true that he was Son, and as he learned this he was freed from a condition of ignorance. As he learned that God was Father, his own Father, he was freed of all the constricting ways of relating to God that the majority of his contemporaries were bound up in. The truth was that between him and God there existed a relationship that could not be duplicated—that he was the only Son of his Father, in other words. He learned many other things about his person and mission, and each new moment of understanding dissipated the darkness that had held fast the eyes of other would-be seers. The kind of freedom he enjoyed, therefore, was a freedom which came from truth—not truth thought about, conjured up, argued over, but truth responded to, lived, experienced. He committed himself to do the truth he knew, to live the truth about himself that he was given to see, and to become who he was in his Father's eyes.

He did not live on once-and-for-all truths, the way an ideologue lives on an ideology. The Spirit did not impart static truths to Jesus about himself, God, and others. The truth he learned was relational, and its continuance, actualization and depth were contingent upon his committing himself to and maintaining the relationships his eyes began to perceive in the living of them. He was made privy to the kind of self-knowledge that made him a seeker for the fullness of a truth he did not yet possess, not a settler for what he already had come to know. There was always more to know about himself, his Father, his brothers and sisters. This teacher never grew too tall to learn. So the abiding Spirit never became expendable. (Although John records him saying, "The Father and I are one," Jesus could have exclaimed, with equal conviction, "The Spirit and I are one.")

Consider the kind of truth he shares with others in the Gospel accounts. It is never prepackaged but always seems to rise out of the situation confronting him or the persons needing him or the questions being posed to him or the animus being shown him. His words come from one who is living life fully, not someone who is just thinking about it. What he says is accessible to those who are immersed in living, giving, loving, losing. Intellectual acumen does not seem to be a prerequisite for understanding him. If anything, it seems to be an obstacle for some of his hearers. In a word, the truth he shares with others is the truth of his own person. (And the archetypal promise he makes to men is that he will send them the selfsame Spirit to teach them the truth about him and themselves that will make them free.)

He acts as one who is at home in himself, in possession of the truth about himself, free to be who he sees himself to be. Enormous pressure was exerted upon him to live according to another understanding of himself than the one he entertained. He resisted that pressure even to the point of dying. In a sense, the whole mission of Jesus came down to this: He couldn't deny and he wouldn't betray the truth that freed him. The further inside himself he was led by the Spirit, the more upset and turmoil Jewish society experienced. It was threatened because his indwelling gave him an identity rootage deeper and truer than the ones the majority of public officials lived by. The officials knew that if he were allowed to go on unimpeded, speaking the truths which were internal to his experience of indwelling, the people would begin to re-examine the most primal elements that held their society together—the image of God preached to them, the image of themselves they had arrived at, and the image of the relationship of Israel to the rest of the nations. "If we let him go on this way everybody will believe in him, and the Romans will come and destroy this Holy Place and our nation" (John 11:48).

Was Jesus free to make a lesser commitment than the one he made? It does not seem that we can give anything more than a hypothetical response to this question. Certainly he must have been free about the degree and manner of his commitment; otherwise, our redemption would somehow have been cajoled from him, and that certainly is unacceptable. He must have entertained ideas about different ways he might relate to his Father. He must have imagined different degrees of union with him. Had he related to his Father the way the elder son in the parable of the two sons related to him, that would not have involved his heart or his self-donation. Had he been the elder son, his commitment could have been more superficial, one in which he was merely obedient to the law. But given what the Spirit taught him about his specialness as far as his Father was concerned, such a response would have been niggardly. The degree of self-communication and love the Father was making evident to Jesus called for a response in kind. Self-donation called for *and got* self-donation. Anything less, I imagine, would have been repugnant to his Father and unacceptable to Jesus. As the story turns out and we come to know who Jesus is, anything less than self-donation would have been as metaphysically unlikely as divorce proceedings beginning within the Trinity itself.

We have already adverted to the fact that his commitment was neither instantaneous nor automatic, and we should add here that it was not irreversible. The freedom of choice that he formally adverted to at the end of his life, that he was laying down his life of his own accord—that same freedom operated in all the prior stages of his life also. His was an ever-unfolding *fiat* given in the face of an ever-developing light about his person and mission. His response was always a matter of choice—love-driven, of course, but choice nonetheless. The final free act of self-donation wherein he delivered himself over into the hands of violent men, grew out of the long series of free choices that went back to the beginning of the process of his individuation as a person. If choice is central to loving, choosing again and again is essential to love's deepening and continuing. No human being can totalize being-in-love once and for all. We wind down physically, emotionally, psychically, intellectually, spiritually. There are always the green wood and the dry in human life, good days and bad. This was no less so for Jesus, whose choice to fully respond to his Father in love could not have been a once-and-for-all thing. It was ever new because it was being continually repeated, renewed, remade.

Was Jesus committed to Israel as such? As a Jew, he would have had to be. His response to Yahweh would have been in terms of, and because of, Yahweh's having entered into a covenantal relationship with Israel. Jesus

111

could hardly be committed to Yahweh and indifferent to the people with whom Yahweh had entered into a covenant relationship. The Gospels never show him to be nonchalant about Israel. He taught and wept over his people; he resisted taking his message outside of their borders; he upbraided them and finally died for them (though not exclusively). This was as it should have been, since these were the people, after all, of the promises that had been first made to Abraham. Their response in faith to Yahweh created a dynamic, ever-changing context within which their individual commitments were evoked, received, and nurtured. If the individual Israelite matured religiously, then more and more of his heart and soul and mind loved the Lord his God and his neighbor as himself. Depending on their spiritual condition, therefore, individually and collectively, they renewed and recreated or diminished the context in which the subsequent generation made its commitments.

But as Jesus was to learn to his great dismay, the social context of the Israel within which he first learned about God and heard his word, was not simply a product of Israel's response to Yahweh. It was a crazy quilt of fidelity and infidelity. Those who identified least closely with the official religion and the religion of the officials were, paradoxically, the most open to hearing God's words on the lips of Jesus. Those, in turn, who seemed the most committed to the religion of Israel were those who showed themselves deaf to Jesus' words and blind to the signs he was working in their midst. He had, to his sorrow, therefore, to develop a discriminating attitude toward Israel, a *yes but* attitude. Toward its authorities he lived what he taught: "According to their words do ye; according to their works do ye not." He would not allow his own response to God to be compromised by the widespread betrayal of the meaning of the covenant in the response to it that he found in much of Israel. Hence, his need to begin to differentiate the relationship he had with Israel. We can see in the Gospels the nuances his relationship to Israel had to take. He never gave up on the people his Father was calling to himself; he could not, since he was one of them. But they gave up on him and asked the Romans to dispose of him so that his atypical relationship with Yahweh might be banished forever from their midst.

Somewhat the same observations might be made about the law. Jesus was not committed to observing the law, but the law he observed was an expression of his love of the one to whom he was committed. The law enhanced his ability to love God and people and afforded innumerable occasions for him to show his love; but his commitment was not to the impersonal law. Official Israel dissipated much of its religious energies in the interpretation of the law and in creating complex ways of trying to apply it to life. But since the focus of Jesus' commitment to God was not on the law, as theirs was, he was free enough from it to observe it, suspend it or transcend it. Torah was only a partial expression of his Father's will for him, and, therefore, its observance was an incomplete way of manifesting the direction of the primordial flow of his being.

Early on, Jesus invited followers to join him so that they could learn how to respond in the enthusiastic way he did to his Father. Gradually he came to realize that there was more to companionship with him than was entailed in a rabbi's relationship with his students. For one thing, he would have been able to see from the nonresponse to him, nonresponse to his Father. This was widespread throughout supposedly religious Israel, he painfully came to see. By contrast, in the effects he had on his followers he would have known that Yahweh was doing a new thing in him, and in them through him. Jesus saw how the law had been perverted by disbelief posturing as belief, and he came to the realization that this form of Yahweh's covenant with Israel would have to change. In time, he realized that he was to be the agent of that change. The new form of commitment to Yahweh would become the following of God's only Son. He was to be the new form of Yahweh's commitment to Israel. And fellowship with him was the new form of people's commitment to God. The person of Jesus was what was new about the new covenant.

All of this did not come together fully until the night before he died. Then the full meaning of the new form of God's commitment to man would be revealed. "When the hour came, he took his place at table . . . then he took some bread and when he had given thanks, broke it and gave it to them saying, 'this is my body which will be given for you; do this as a memorial of me.' He did the same with the cup after supper and said, 'This cup is the new covenant in my blood which will be poured out for you'" (Luke 22:14–20). Ultimately, following him meant intimacy in his own life as a result of his death. The new bond between God and humankind, and the new form of the commitment to Yahweh were to be Christ himself—his own life symbolized by bread and wine.

Just as the Father's commitment to his Son is most manifest in Jesus' resurrection, so in the crucifixion scene the meaning par excellence of the mystery of Jesus' commitment stands forth. Here is complete self-donation, a life freely and completely given. It is an act of total trust and risk, but most of all it is an act of love of those with whom he was in communion—his Father and his friends. The Gospel is at pains to show that the dark underside of suffering, ignominy and death is the superficial side of the mystery. Underneath the evidence of life poured out is ascension to the fullness of life. What looks like descent into the realm of death is ascent into perfect communion as the last traces of disunion with his Father and his friends fall away. His glory is at its highest when his self-donation is at its fullest. The ultimate comment on this scene and the final significance of commitment is Jesus' own words: "He who loses his life will find it" (Mark 8:35). We should be able to hear in these words and see in this act the meaning of love and commitment of ourselves to one another.

Chapter V
Some New Testament Commitments

Some people might object that the observations made in the previous chapter about commitment are all very well and good if one is divine. But since few feel that they personally enjoy that status, there is a question of how the matter in the preceding chapter could pertain to the rest of us. An objection such as this is inevitable if one cannot perceive Jesus as one of us in all things save sin. If one can, then he will believe that in Jesus' commitment we can see more fully into our own, that in his commitment we can see implications and consequences we do not yet see or experience in our own. Furthermore, he did not keep his own experience of commitment to himself but made it an essential part of his teaching. He did so because he believed that what he was capable of others would also be capable of, both with respect to God and to one another.

He taught others only what he himself had learned, and

invited others to live only what he himself was alive to. With regard to commitment, recall how much he cherished and advocated single-mindedness and his *caveat* about serving two masters. Or his parable about the pearl of great price. Selling many things to purchase the one thing prized most of all encapsules Jesus' own experience of commitment. Having made that transaction, everything else was simply an expression of his primordial commitment. That was why he could enthuse over the widow who deposited her penny in the temple treasury. Like him, the simplest gesture told where her heart was.

By way of contrast, think of the wrath that the master in the parable of the talents visited on the head of the servant who recoiled from committing himself and hid his talent. He would not risk losing what he had been given. He would not commit himself, so he "went off, dug a hole in the ground and hid his master's money" (Matt. 25:18). For not allowing what he had received to increase and grow, the servant is banished from the joyous household of the master. Ironically, he is consigned to the same static darkness that he had reserved for his master's gift to him. By risking nothing in order to retain what he had, his noncommitment left him in a condition of spirit in which he was only half alive.

Or take the man with the grain surplus who decided to pull down his narrow barns and build bigger ones. He made a commitment, as it were, but it was to himself and to the procurement of his own comfort. He is called "fool" in the Gospel for his self-absorption. "My soul, you have plenty of good things laid by for many years to come. Take things easy, eat, drink and have a good time." Since

117

the purview of his choice is merely himself, "this very night demand will be made for your soul" (Luke 12:19–20).

Although Jesus invited some people to follow him, he did not trust commitments made to him that were initiated, uninvited, by would-be followers. As he and his disciples were making their way toward Jerusalem, someone said to Jesus, "I will be your follower wherever you go" (Luke 9:57). Rather than feeling elation at what seemed to be so unconditional a response to him, Jesus ignored the zealot and used the occasion to describe his own condition of life. "The foxes have holes and the birds of the air, nests, but the Son of man has nowhere to lay his head" (Luke 9:58). Jesus' source of security, if we can call it that, did not repose in anything earthly or structural or institutional. The precondition for living the kind of life that Jesus lived was that he be willing to walk into the future supported only by the experience of indwelling. That was the way he walked into it. His renunciation of the most basic material security—namely, lodging—symbolizes this, I believe. Jesus indicated to this would-be follower that "follow me" meant living in the manner of indwelling in which he lived, which is beyond security, beyond certainties, beyond definitions. Seeking first the one thing necessary for life as he saw it, he found that "all these other things will be given you as well" (Matt. 6:33).

Another would-be follower indicated his firm intention to leave all for companionship with Jesus. But first, he had to clear up one seemingly slight detail: "Let me take leave of my people at home" (Luke 9:61). This, according to Luke, was the occasion for Jesus' responding: "Once the hand is laid to the plow no one who looks back is fit for the kingdom of God" (Luke 9:62). Jesus was saying something about himself here—something about the straight line of his own commitment. He knew where he had come from and where he was going. The kingdom of God which he was proclaiming and manifesting orients the one who is committed to pursuing its promise with the same unidirectional intent as the farmer whose plow is directed toward a single distant point and who, for that reason, can furrow a straight row.

About the intentions of these two would-be followers to commit themselves to Jesus, this might be said in general. Jesus' commitment to his Father was not generated by him any more than his own life was self-generated. He would not, therefore, entertain the prospect of having followers whose commitment to him was due to their own choice. "You have not chosen me but I have chosen you" (John 15:16) shows something unique about the Christian's commitment to God in Christ and suggests something about what is ideal in other interpersonal commitments also. It should not be produced by willing it. Its origins are not to be found in the will of the would-be follower of Christ in the first case, nor in the will of the would-be committer in other interpersonal commitments. Ideally it is a choosing that has its origins in the experience of indwelling.

A CLASSIC CASE OF NONCOMMITMENT

There is a classic case of noncommitment recorded by all three Synoptics (Matt. 19, Mark 10, Luke 18) that teaches us much about interpersonal commitment as well as commitment to Christ. The person in question is without a name, suggesting perhaps that he can also be a type representing more than himself. For example, he could be taken as representative of the noncommitment of Israel itself. Called only a man by all three evangelists, he is given the added description in Matthew and Mark of being "a man of great wealth" and "a member of one of the leading families" by Luke. He is concerned with eternal life and, therefore, has enough religious discontent and need to approach the respected teacher Jesus with the question: "What is still necessary for me to inherit or possess eternal life?" In order to gauge the man's religious condition Jesus uses the measure of his obedience to the basic commandments of God. The man confesses that he has kept all these since his youth. No small feat, and one would think reason for rejoicing and a bit of praise or at least encouragement to hang in there. But no such response is forthcoming from Jesus. As usual, he sees something beyond the surface, something deeper than the level of the man's performance or constancy.

On the basis of what is said next we can surmise what Jesus discerns about the man's religious condition. There was obedience but it was religiously superficial. At a deeper level the man was keeping his heart to himself while stockpiling righteousness points by observing observances and avoiding trespasses. His religious condition involved his feet but did not involve his heart. He was not giving himself in trust and love to God; he was keeping and adding to his own righteousness record and acting as the broker of his own salvation. Somewhere along the line, the process that began to flow toward self-donation from him to others and to God was diverted and turned back into himself. Jesus concluded that for the man to crack through the walls within which he had become inured, he would have to get rid of his material wealth.

The man had come to treat spiritual realities the same way he dealt with his considerable wealth. He stockpiled both, putting his trust in the things he had amassed, whether spiritual or material, rather than in God. Something was radically wrong, but unable to put his finger on it, he sought out Jesus. And Jesus decided on a radical, two-edged solution. He issued a remarkable invitation: Follow me.

I don't believe that this was a religious journey as such that Jesus was asking the man to undertake. He knew he had to be led away from this wrongheaded source of security and that he had to resituate the center of his trust. To begin the process of self-donation he had to entrust himself to another at least enough to walk with him. By such a gesture, the man of great wealth would be saying at least to himself that his worth was in his person rather than in the spiritual and material wealth he had amassed and hoped to preserve. If he was willing to go baggageless and walk with another, he would be at least *in via* to doing so with the Other. With his eye on another, someone beyond himself, he would eventually find a treasure outside himself, and if that step were successfully traversed he could come to the point of entrusting himself to God in love and faith, he could find his treasure in heaven rather than where it was now. The journey toward his own salvation had to begin with an act of trust, a stepping out beyond his own self-absorption. That is to say, companionship could lead to the gift of himself in love to another, who in this instance was Jesus. The process of self-donation ultimately leads to eternal life, Jesus was telling him. But self-transcendence through self-donation was only one part of Jesus' solution.

Even as he was recommending such a vulnerable stepping forth, Jesus knew another action was necessary. There was a material aspect to the man's sorry spiritual condition which both symbolized and reinforced that condition. Hence, the other part of Jesus' solution was the invitation to "sell all you have and give the money to the poor." It seems that Jesus is saying several things by such a directive. For one thing, someone who would entrust himself to and follow another must first of all esteem himself. A sure sign of personal disesteem is the need to tote around with oneself the baggage of possessions or credentials or performance charts to camouflage one's felt emptiness either before God or man. It is as if Jesus is saying: "If you're going to accompany me, the center of your trust must move off of things and onto persons—first of all yourself and, in turn, me and ultimately the personal God who is the source of all good things." Not that one's salvation is guaranteed by this first step. (Think of one of Jesus' followers who had already begun to walk with Jesus at the time the rich young man came forward, but who eventually reverted to putting his trust on something a little more tangible than companionship with Jesus and membership in the kingdom that Jesus preached. I am of course thinking of the one who finally betrayed him, Judas Iscariot.) Jesus knew that what this rich young man decided to do about his possessions, which were preventing his spirit from loving God and man, would determine whether he could be a fit subject for eternal life, which was meant to begin in time.

This brief episode tells us something about Jesus' insight into the nature of religion and its intimate connection with commitment. The attempt to be religious without commiting oneself to another or others can end up with one using religion, God, and others to serve oneself. Jesus had apparently little or nothing by way of material possessions and he had no use for, and accorded no value to, religious observances that were done with an eye to gaining merits. On the other hand, the act of serving another, loving another, being present to another, walking with another, any act whereby one went out from himself to the other, was highly valued in Jesus' eyes. Consequently, Jesus would have this man begin with the simplest act of risking, committing himself to walk with him in companionship and away from the support systems he had constructed for himself. He did not accept the invitation. He was willing to be taught and he was docile up to a point, but he wanted the whole process of receiving eternal life to take place without his having to leave himself. He wanted his redemption to take place internally. He wanted to know more and grow more in righteousness by observance. But lose his footing, give himself, come out from himself, yield to a life of love or even the first faint hints of it? No! He decided against following another, against detaching himself from the sources of his security. He decided against life and risk and for self-absorption. "And he went away sad" (Matt. 19:22).

Several observations should be appended here to our reflections on this incident. The intimate interplay between redemption and relationship, damnation and isolation, could hardly be more evident than it is in this incident. And the obstructionist influence of wealth, whether material or religious, to making an interpersonal commitment, even so slight a commitment as companionship with and presence to another, is also evident here. Jesus seems almost to groan in pain as the man of wealth turns away. In his lament he observes to his followers: "How hard it is for those who have riches to enter the kingdom of heaven" (Mark 10:23). How much easier, on the other hand, for tax gatherers and harlots who have no pretensions or religious wealth to preserve to enter the kingdom of heaven.

One could also pause here to see the wisdom of God in the incarnation of his Son. God had made man in the image of himself out of the overflow of his own internal life of love. But if God was internally triune, eternally a Trinity in which each of the divine persons was unique insofar as self-donation was a constitutive aspect of the reality of each, then one who was made in God's image would presumably be the same. But that meant he would be incomplete until and unless he lost his footing in the gift of himself to the Other. The Other whom the human person was made for was God himself, but without a more immediate recipient of his self-donation, self-absorption was too proximate a possibility. And so God gave him one who was "bone from his bone and flesh from his flesh" (Gen. 2:23) because God saw that "it is not good that the man should be alone" (Gen. 2:18). When that little scheme did not work out the way God had intended it, he gave us another, who was also bone of our bone and flesh of our flesh, to bridge the chasm that sin had created. Hence, the incarnation. That a chasm existed is obvious from this incident of the rich young man.

The summation of Jesus' teaching on commitment took

the form of a commandment: "Love one another as I have loved you." Commit yourselves to one another in love! By determining on this single, new commandment, the observance of which he hoped would bring attention to his little community throughout the world, Jesus shows how well he understood himself as well as his brothers and sisters. Otherwise, under the impetus of his crucifixion and resurrection, his ascension and the descent of the Spirit upon the community, he could envision his followers zooming off into a spiritualization of commitment. He could see them arriving at a degree of fervor in which they would ignore loving one another in the name of God, ignore their bodies and the human condition in the name of the Spirit, disregard their families and communities in the name of the Gospel and mission. By putting the highest priority on love of one another, however, Jesus sought to root their lives and their words in reality; their commitment to God was to be enfleshed in their relationships with one another, and the redemption of each follower was to be expressed at the nitty-gritty level of self-donation. He knew that they could easily miss the point of a kingdom that was being born from above, so he preached a kingdom of persons whose hearts were being given to God ultimately but to one another proximately. Their love behavior toward each other was to be the omnipresent sign of the primordial commitment their hearts were making.

I believe that the New Testament has much more to say about interpersonal commitments. We will try to ferret this out by continuing with the process we decided to follow in the fourth chapter—that is, by taking actual instances of commitment and seeking to reflect on the mystery of it in terms of these. The first of these will be with the mother of Jesus.

MARY'S COMMITMENT

Anyone who has delved into the complex question about the historical core of the Gospels (as distinguished from the theological understanding which the community added to this core) is familiar with the terminology of "the Jesus of history" versus "the Christ of faith." They would likewise be aware that these two aspects of Christology are not as dissociable from one another as scholars had initially hoped. In fact, there were practically as many opinions about what belonged to the historical core and what belonged to the theological additions to that core as there were exegetes and theologians who studied the question. We might say the same thing about Jesus' mother. There is an enormous body of scholarship on the difference between the Mary of history and the mother of God, or the theological additions about her life which were articulated in function of the Christologies that the evangelists developed.

Since we are interested in what the Scriptures can teach us about the meaning of commitment in the life of Mary, our purposes are both modest and quite specific and need not get us into the historical question. We will look at the preveneration Mary, Mary of the Gospels, in terms of her commitment to God and her son and her people.

The first thing that must strike one is the bewildering evolution Mary's commitment to God underwent in the brief span of her lifetime. In her early years, like any other Jew, her commitment to God would have had its contents determined by the law taught her by her elders and the practices of piety inculcated by her family and synagogue. She would also have come to know the ways of the God of Abraham, Isaac and Jacob by her attentive listening to the reading of the Scriptures in the synagogue. As she matured, attentiveness to his word became characteristic of Mary, though she learned to listen for it in places other than Scripture. Several times in the New Testament she is described as "pondering in her heart" the words she hears on the lips of men and angels. She becomes a ponderer of events also. For all she knew, her commitment to God was to be bodied forth for the rest of her life by personal prayer, fidelity to religious observances, obedience to the law, attentiveness to the word of God, and the love of her parents and neighbors.

But with the annunciation, the manner of her commitment to God changed radically. Although the above-mentioned practices continued, her commitment would now be shown by her attentiveness to her son. In this she was like any woman who becomes a mother. But there was a big difference. Insofar as her son was unlike any other baby or child or adolescent or man who ever lived, her commitment to God was much more fully embodied by her care of him than has ever been the case with any other mother. Jesus became the immediate recipient of the self-donation which she had always directed toward Yahweh. Not that it was not still directed to the God of Abraham, Isaac, and Jacob, but her son stood inside that divine presence in a way that she would not be able to fully comprehend even after years of pondering.

She must have come close to being scandalized by the

annunciation, since the God of Judaism was so wholly Other, so transcendent and awesome and now so immanent and intimate. She is described by Luke as being "deeply disturbed" (Luke 1:29) upon hearing the words that made his presence so immediate and his will so particular. She could not have known at the time the full implications of what God had in mind for her or her son; she could not have dreamed at that moment what the Christian community came to believe—that the Word that was made flesh in her womb was with God from the beginning and that that Word was God. Although she could not have known this, she would have known that she was being asked to accept a new horizon by acceding to the news that the angel announced to her. She was being asked to make and she freely, if bewilderingly, determined on an act of vertical freedom.

After the nativity the form of her commitment to Yahweh was still framed by the law, although there was now also a special baby in the center of it. We can see this both in the circumcision, which took place eight days after his birth, and in the purification, which took place forty days after that. Both of these rites were prescribed by the law of Moses. There is continuity with the past and yet discontinuity in the ways that her commitment to God are expressed. And in the thousand days of his youth, when he was subject to her and Joseph in Nazareth, we have every reason to believe that the form of her commitment to God would have remained a mixture of both new things and old. As her son matured, her commitment to him changed in its expression. The time came when he had to go away from her to proclaim a kingdom the outlines of which were probably very indistinct to her (and to him). It would have been easier for her if her commitment to him had fixated so that she could relate to him according to the way she saw him at any one stage in their relationship. But she persevered in relating to him in his becoming, she acceded to his developing self-understanding which necessitated his leaving her for the unknown, and for this she is worthy of great praise.

A commitment to a person can never fixate on what one has been without ceasing to be a commitment to that person. It is then a commitment to the image that one entertains of the other, or it is a commitment to oneself and one's needs. In this connection it is significant that Mary showed her fidelity to Jesus not so much by what she said or by the actions she undertook. It is mainly by her presence that she showed herself faithful to him. Recall the places she was present, in his public life, according to the Gospel accounts of her life. There was Cana, the beginning of the signs, where he "let his glory be seen" (John 2:12) and where his disciples first came to believe in him. And when the signs reached their zenith, at the crucifixion, "near the cross of Jesus stood his mother" (John 19:25). And when his followers themselves were about to become a new sign, that is to say, after his ascension and before the descent of the Spirit upon them, while they were all joined in continuous prayer, there was "Mary, the mother of Jesus" in their midst (Acts 1:14).

Faithfulness was not a quality that would have flowered naturally from Mary's character or temperament any more than it does from anyone's. Its origins are not natural at all, but are to be found in God's faithfulness. Because she had known and loved Yahweh from her earliest years, her life was a reflection of his qualities, chief of which was his faithful love, as he never tired of reminding Israel. Mary's life therefore magnified this characteristic. The whole Magnificat is a paean of praise to Yahweh for his faithfulness both to Israel, his servant, as well as to his lowly handmaid. "All generations will call me blessed for the Almighty has done great things for me" (chief of which is that he has made me faithful to him) "and holy is his name" (Luke 1:48–49). Steadfast fidelity in any commitment is a reflection of the faithfulness of the author of all fidelity, as we shall see subsequently.

If she could have felt scandal at the annunciation about God's ways with men, imagine the scandal Mary must have felt when she saw the response that many gave to her son—when she saw the need of Israel's leaders to find her son guilty so that they could get on with their business-as-usual ways that allowed them to traffic in godware. But I wonder if anything, in her years with her son, could have prepared her for what her commitment to God was to mean as a result of Pentecost. If her first *fiat* required her to change horizons, what must that one have involved? Recall that that event, the descent of the Holy Spirit upon her and the community of believers, would have revealed something about her son that his birth, life, death, and resurrection never did. "No one can say, 'Jesus is Lord' except he is under the influence of the Holy Spirit" (I Cor. 12:3). Did she ever pronounce the word "Lord" of her own son while she was here on earth? One who was as intimate to her as her own womb and as dependent on her body as a fetus was now being pronounced Lord of the universe, was now believed to have power equal to God himself. If we can take Mary off the goddess shelf that a centuries-old Latin Catholicism has put her on, we can comprehend how disconcerting these changing horizons of her commitment to God must have been, most of all this last one in which her son becomes acclaimed Lord. She would have had to ponder God's fidelity at length to see a continuity to his plan—a plan in which she must revere every jot and tittle of the law that she had known and lived from her youth, and at the same time proclaim her son Lord. Her own fidelity to God required a number of horizon shifts and vertical exercises of freedom.

But Mary's life illustrates something about commitment in relationship to the community that is also important. She must have been keenly tempted at any one point, starting with the annunciation invitation, to confine her responses to God to those which were respected, accept-able and expected of her by the community of Israel. Had they not, after all, taught her her faith, her prayers, what to believe in, what Israel was, and what the covenant meant? If she had even in the slightest degree used what she had learned about God, even unconsciously, as a way of fitting into the community rather than being in union with God, she would never have said "yes" to the invita-tion to conceive and bear a son whose life was to be like a sword piercing her soul (Luke 2:35).

In subtle ways religion can become a means of uniting with men rather than God. In the name of the community one can easily shirk the personal commitment that God calls each individual to. It is easier to live in a way that says, "Be it done unto me according to the *community's* word" than to say, "Be it done unto me according to *your* word," as Mary said. Even commitments made out of the purest motives can gradually become subordinate to con-

131

SHOULD ANYONE SAY FOREVER?

siderations of how others might react and what they might expect. This is a subtle temptation, to put the onus for spelling out the intrinsic content of God's call to the individual onto the community. The parameters of the Jewish and Christian communities were meant to be enriched by the unique response of each believing individual to God's word as it is spoken to him, heard by him, and grows in him uniquely. The classical description of this aspect of the Christian economy was penned by Paul in his doctrine on the individual charismata which, taken together, are to produce a gift-laden and enriching community. Mary's life has much to say about the truth of this.

Up to a point she is shaped by the community, by the community, that is, that she grew up in and by the overarching commitment to Yahweh that that community had made. But while she was still young, she had to proceed by herself, unconfirmed by that same community, to make a gift of herself to God, a gift that was quite different from what any other Jewish girl had ever been asked to make. In her case, not only was she not confirmed by the community, but by her *fiat* she put herself in the proximate occasion of being condemned by that community. "Joseph, being a man of honor . . . decided to divorce her" (Matt. 1:19). How much easier it would have been for her simply to say "no" and then peacefully repose on the context of belief in God which surrounded her—a context, after all, that had been created by God's chosen people and their belief in him. How much easier it would have been for her to do this and then preen herself on her fidelity to God. Mary is a good example of the unique nature of each person's commitment. She is also a reminder of the difficulty we should experience about judging another's fidelity or infidelity. The same inviolability with which we reverence each other's consciences must also be accorded each individual's commitments.

A final thing can be learned about commitment from the life of Mary. Hope is essential to every commitment. But it was particularly internal to those commitments which were built on the awaited Messiah. Since she was Jewish, Mary learned from her earliest days to be future-oriented. She lived in hope, entertaining great expectations about what her God would do in, and through, the Messiah whom he would send to his people. Long before she knew that she would be asked to play so critical a role in his coming, she lived in restless expectation of the Messiah whom Israel awaited. She was as filled with expectation that God's power would break forth in, through and over Israel as she was with love of him. Her ability to live fully in the present while at the same time seeing that the present contains merely a hint of what is still to come resplendently, derives from a power that classical theology would one day call the infused virtue of hope. This does not mean that her life became hope-filled without her active nurturing of the virtualities of this infused gift. Living in hope took on new dimensions, of course, with the actual coming of the Messiah.

Those who began to follow him also began to see, howsoever indistinctly, that what they were awaiting was being focused by him. The kingdom he was preaching was the kingdom they had awaited. And little by little they could see that that same kingdom was being localized in his person. There is good reason to believe that

Mary saw all of this long before anyone else did. The only words placed on the lips of Mary by the evangelist (apart from the infancy narratives) are: "Do whatever he tells you" (John 2:5). This was the instruction she gave to the servants at the wedding feast in Cana. If there is a historical core to the incident, these words would suggest that her Messianic expectations had already begun to focus on her son.

The virtue of hope that Mary enjoyed gave her the power to see that the present was already pregnant with the final times. What was still to come was confirmed by what was already here, though only in seed, in foretaste, and in first fruits.

Imagine what Mary's life would have been like without hope. Her commitment to God would not have opened out to the future but would have fixated on the past. Her prayer would not have been open to surprises but would largely have been a re-enactment and a recollection of God's past interventions celebrated in an increasingly stylized way. Although she was affected in the deepest roots of her being by her past, her commitment was future oriented; it was to the ever-living God who was continually breaking into the present through the expectations of what was still to come that he instilled hope in the hearts of his people.

You don't have to be Jewish to be a hope-er. Mary's commitment to Yahweh illustrates what must be true of all interpersonal commitments. They will be lived more in hope than in full possession of what was hoped for when the commitment was made. Commitments persist, even thrive, if what was hoped for is present in some measure. They diminish if nothing that was hoped for is realized. A commitment that is hopeless will cease to be, even though the shell remains for years. One way for new life to be breathed into dispirited commitments is to try to revive the hopes that were once entertained of them.

PAUL'S COMMITMENT

The things we have learned thus far from the actual examples of New Testament commitments are not, as far as I am concerned, pious thoughts to be pasted on to what we saw in the first part of our study. They are rather essential to perceiving more fully the structure, nature, and mystery of interpersonal commitment. St. Paul's experience is a further illustration of still other aspects about the nature of commitment not touched in the previous instances.

His life is one long, unswerving commitment to God, but in two radically different ways. The difference between these two should be instructive. Paul was no less committed to God at the height of his career when he was persecuting Christians than he was proclaiming Christ crucified, and yet he was a totally different man. This is meant simply as an observation, not a religious judgment or a theological statement. In Paul we can see the import of a commitment that has been refocused. The object of Paul's commitment remained the same, namely God himself. But a change in how that object is viewed was the remaking of the viewer. The theological reason behind the change has ultimately nothing to do with Paul. It has to do with the new relationship that God established between himself and humankind in Christ, but Paul was made privy to that more intimate relationship. The philosophical reason for the change that took place in Paul is that the objects of our commitments operate as final causes, flowing into the one who has made them and affecting the whole direction and texture of his being. He becomes something he would not have been if he had not so committed himself. That something different depends on what and who it is that he has committed himself to.

Yahweh was Saul of Tarsus' God. He served him unstintingly through his observance of the law and through works of supererogation. The New Testament suggests that there is a congruence between the kind of person Saul of Tarsus was and the kind of God Saul of Tarsus served. Not Yahweh as he is in himself, mind you, but Yahweh according to the understanding Saul had of him. Saul's God had an either/or absoluteness about him, a trait which, when made visible in the person of Saul, struck terror into those that Saul saw as the enemy—that is to say, Christians. Given this image, there was never a question of this God's accommodating himself to persons, if in so doing the truth of the Torah would be compromised. Saul's God was also an exclusivist who dealt harshly with those who were beyond the pale of Judaism. Like his God, Saul worked indefatigably six days a week (especially at the interpretation and observance of the law), and on the seventh day he rested, totally, except for whatever energy it took to observe those who might be breaking the sabbath. (He made note of such transgressions, as he was sure his God did also.) It does not seem that there was much room for spontaneity in his life, though his behavior could be perfected *sine fine*. The immediate content of Saul's commitment involved knowing what the law was and the most recent interpretation of it, and then observing it. The power to fulfill the law came from oneself. Though this may sound judgmental, it is the way Paul judged himself when he looked back upon his life. What he did not say and did not realize was that he was a Yahweh in miniature, unwittingly, unintentionally. You become what you love and commit yourself to—or, to be more precise, what your image is of the one you commit yourself to. (This image, of course, was not what or who Yahweh actually was; it was the way interpreters and Paul had distorted him.)

The Yahweh that Saul of Tarsus served doesn't tell us much about the God of Abraham, Isaac, and Jacob, but it does tell us a lot about the importance of a person's focus, the image he has of God or of another person he commits himself to. I believe this is what the Psalmist meant when he observed that people end up like the gods they fashion for themselves. Contrasting commitment to Yahweh with the absurdity of the pagans fashioning their own objects of commitment, Psalm 115 says: ". . . their idols, in silver and gold, [are] products of human skill, have mouths, but never speak, eyes, but never see, ears but never hear, noses but never smell, hands but never touch, feet but never walk, and not a sound from their throats. Their makers will end up like them, and so will anyone who relies on them."

The radical nature of Paul's commitment to Jesus shines through every page of his epistles, but perhaps no more clearly can it be seen than in a few of the verses in the third chapter of his letter to the Philippians: "For Christ Jesus, my Lord and I have accepted the loss of everything, and I look on everything as so much rubbish. If only I can have Christ and be given a place in Him . . .

all I want is to know Christ and the power of His resurrection and to share his sufferings by reproducing the pattern of His death . . . I have not yet won, but I am still running, trying to capture the prize for which Christ captured me . . . I forget the past and I strain ahead for what is to come; I am racing for the finish for the prize for which God calls us upward to receive in Christ Jesus" (Phil. 3:8–15).

Paul literally lost his footing in trust, hope, belief, and love of the person of Christ Jesus. A dramatic relationship began to take place between Paul and Jesus after the interruption of Saul's journey on the road to Damascus. The best adjective one could use to describe the interpersonal intimacy of that relationship is symbiotic. A symbiotic relationship is one in which two living entities live as if they were one. Certainly the union between Paul and Christ was more than a moral one, for that would simply indicate that two wills functioned as one—though that was part of it. And it was more than an affective union, which would only mean that Paul's heart was caught up with the attractiveness of Christ Jesus—though that was part of it, too. "Symbiotic" seems to be a better term for their union than indwelling because, by the free choice of both, another's spirit was permeating Paul's own. The life of Paul was now unfolding in the life of another, and the life of the other was unfolding in the life of Paul. Paul was allowing the very core of his own spirit to be penetrated by the Spirit of Jesus. So complete is the permeation that Paul can say: "I live now not I, but Christ lives within me" (Gal. 2:20). This is not an announcement of Paul's annihilation or the dilution of his personality. It is a confession of the degree of compenetration that Paul had freely allowed to take place in his life. This resembles the new condition of being that was described elsewhere as indwelling.

Just as Saul of Tarsus had taken on the qualities of the one whom he had served, so Paul the apostle began to take on the qualities of the one to whom he gave himself in love. Although many qualities could be chosen to illustrate this, we will reflect on just one of the ways in which Paul begins to resemble Jesus. Paul's freedom is reminiscent of the freedom of Christ Jesus.

We begin to see the chains fall away from his person. The particularisms that had bound Paul in the past no longer held him. The most evident is a geographical one, as we see him plowing the seas to the four corners of the known earth to proclaim the one he believes in and has entrusted himself to. We see the shackles of an observance-centered piety fall away from Paul as he proclaims in a universe suddenly turned benign: "For me there are no forbidden things" (I Cor. 10:23). He refuses to allow his freedom in Christ to be limited by others' hangups and unfreeing categories. "Why should my freedom depend on someone else's conscience?" he wonders (I Cor. 10:29). In the same letter Paul indicates the source of his freedom and why he does not need to be approved by others. A man who has received the gift of the spirit, "is able to judge the value of everything and his own value is not to be judged by other men" (I Cor. 2:15). Fear or self-doubt, or the need to prove himself, or to be approved—these exerted little influence over him, apparently. Like his Master, he defied those authorities who could kill his body. Like his Master, he defied the powers of the seas to quench his spirit. Like his Master, he freely loved others and he did so in anguish and joy and tears. He also freely left them in order to tell others of the Christ in whom he was indwelling. He was free to enter prison while despising the shame of it and boasting about the reason for his incarceration. He was free to risk being ostracized in order to goad whole communities. The last redoubt of Paul's unfreedom, which was Paul himself, that too was conquered by Christ. He described the self-donation he was consciously making as being "poured out like a libation" (II Tim. 4:6).

It is beautiful to see how unashamed of the scandal of the cross Paul was. He proclaims Christ crucified with impunity in the face of those who scorned and found foolish the irony of the life of the Nazarene. Paul was conscious that his own freedom had been purchased by Christ at a very high price; consequently, he was aware of how ridiculous it would have been if he did not enjoy or even suspicion it. Paul was adamant that no one would steal that freedom from him. He knew that to be one with Christ was to be one with the only person who was totally free; so he did not settle for anything less at any point in his life than union with the free and freeing Jesus. It would be instructive to put all his letters together in chronological order to see how his own expansiveness parallels his experience of Christ until his Christology becomes cosmic.

It is tempting to dwell on the theology of what took place between Paul and Jesus, but we do so only to the extent that it is necessary to illuminate the dynamics of interpersonal commitment. The focus of Paul's commitment to God had become the person of Christ Jesus. His commitment to God was emptied of its legal content only to be filled with an immediate and personal content. Paul believed that Jesus was both brother and fellow human being, and at the same time one who was with Yahweh and one in stature with him. Given the fact of the incarnation and the resurrection of Jesus, Paul was able to surrender his whole life to God in a way that he had not been able to do before. Because of the incarnation, Paul (and all men and women) had an immediate personal medium through which he could give himself to God. And God in his own Son had a more intimate way of communicating himself to Paul and the rest of humankind. A Christian believes that because of the incarnation, it is more likely that the process of self-donation that each individual is capable of will be oriented to and terminated in God himself.

If the meaning of commitment is measured by intention or by degree of intensity or will power, then Saul of Tarsus was just as committed as Paul, the apostle to the Gentiles. But if commitment is measured in terms of self-donation, then Paul would have to be seen as enormously more committed than Saul. For Paul entrusted his entire self to the risen one whose own trusting love of his Father made him what he was yesterday, is today, and will be forever.

Paul could never get over the fact that he was seized, grasped, chosen, elected, through no merit of his own. An interesting passivity begins to develop in his life. Not that he is not exhausted by his labors of proclaiming Christ crucified, but these labors do not have their impetus in his need to be religious or win righteousness or achieve perfection. These labors are his response to his having been chosen. Paul is quite conscious of the mystery of it all.

Why me? Why not him or her? He knew that it was not he who made the commitment. It was made by God, and it is for each individual to ratify or reject it. What Paul saw instantaneously usually takes the rest of us a lifetime to perceive, namely that God has chosen us to become one with him in his Son. That is the commitment he is making to us. The initiative is his. It is always and only as a response to God's commitment of himself in Christ that a Christian's commitment derives meaning.

Is being chosen rather than choosing true only of the Christian's commitment to Christ, or does it also hold for other commitments, whether made by Christians or not? As was mentioned before, I believe it holds also for other interpersonal commitments, and that their quality will be relative to whether they are self-generated choices or not. If we transpose the language—that is to say, take it out of its religious connotations—the point could become clear. Either party, in any interpersonal commitment, should be able to say: "Your choice of me is not the stuff that holds our commitment together any more than my choice of you is. The union that we have preceded our choices. We were free to say yes or no to our union, but the fact that we both said and continue to say yes does not produce that union." In other words, interpersonal commitments that are the product of will power are not ideal. The ideal is that interpersonal commitments be rooted in love and ratified in freedom.

Some further things could be derived from this position: (1) The purer the commitment the less is it something one makes and the more is it something one yields to. (2) The purer the self-donation, the less one is focused on making a commitment or having made a commitment or even on the commitment itself. One's "eye" is on the one to whom one gives oneself. (3) Commitments that arise from mutual presence are more likely to be persevered in than those whose roots are voluntaristic.

Paul the apostle illustrates all of these things well. The voluntarism of his days as a member of the Pharisee sect are long since past when he can say: "I live now not I but Christ lives in me." He responded fully to the choice that had been made of him by Christ (rather than by him of Christ). At no point in his life as a Christian did he believe that the source of his commitment was himself. The gift he was given was to see that God was committing himself to him in his Son. Paul had believed in God all his life, as a result of a gift of faith. But it took a new gift for him to see that a new relationship was being knitted together between God and humankind—that a new covenant was coming into being in Christ Jesus, and that he was being called into that new relationship.

Another aspect of Paul's commitment (or now, to be more accurate, his response to God's commitment to him in Christ) that is worth noting is the sense of self-worth on which it is built. Although, as we have already noted, for a person's selfhood to be complete, commitment is essential, nonetheless, if the personality attempting the commitment is indeterminate and the sense of self weak, the commitment cannot help but be unsuccessful. Such a commitment will frequently be used to make up for or supply what the person himself cannot supply, namely, a sense of self-worth. A commitment presumes, as we can see in Paul, that before it can be made there must be a self that is sufficiently coherent and strong that it does not ask the other to take over "the care and feeding" of what it has given up on. It is counterproductive for people to try to overcome a sense of worthlessness through commitments or to ask others to give them a sense of purpose or identity. Self-doubt, or personal disesteem, is an impossible base for self-donation. It makes it more than likely that a person will simulate commitment in the hope that the other will take responsibility for him.

Contrast the impoverished sense of self with Paul's self-esteem—almost arrogance, as it sounds at times. For example, in the letter to the Philippians, Paul indicates how he thinks about himself. "Take any man," he says, "who thinks he can rely on what is physical, and you will see that I am better qualified. I was born of the race of Israel and of the tribe of Benjamin, a Hebrew born of Hebrew parents and I was circumcised when I was eight days old." Which of you is more blue-blood than I, in other words. He proceeds, "as for the law I was a Pharisee," which was a thing of esteem at that time. "As for religious zeal, I was a persecutor of the church. As far as the law can make you perfect, I was faultless" (Phil. 3:4–6).

When Paul falls under the reign of God in Christ he remains this same strong person. The effects of his strong sense of self-worth, complemented now by the abiding union with the Lord, can be felt in the remotest corners of the Christian diaspora. His relationship with Christ is only as strong as his personal sense of self-worth. Christ complements the self of Paul the way a lover complements and completes the beloved. When Paul found a weak sense of self in other people he encouraged them to copy him in his union with God in Christ. Again and again in his letters he encourages those who are weak or unstable, in either their sense of self-worth or their faith, to be "imitators of me as I am of Christ." Paul, however, never despaired of the weak sense of self that he found in so many of his brothers and sisters. He encouraged them to pray for the Spirit, that their hidden selves, their weak selves, their inevident selves might grow strong. For example, in his letter to the Ephesians, he writes: "This then is what I pray . . . out of his infinite glory may he give you the power through his Spirit for your hidden self to grow strong so that Christ may live in your hearts through faith, and then planted in love and built on love you will with all the saints have strength to grasp the breadth and the length, the height and the depth, until knowing the love of Christ which is beyond all knowledge, you are filled with the utter fullness of God" (Eph. 3:14–19).

Notice here that Paul is suggesting that the precondition for being able to grasp the breadth and length, the height and the depth of the love of Christ, is that the hidden self become more evident and strong enough to sustain and be a base for one's commitment. The Spirit's power is to be sought for the purpose of having one's hidden self become more evident and stronger. Paul seemed always to be in touch with his own feelings about himself; his self was evident to him, insofar as that is ever possible to us. He emotes freely in his letters, which presumes that he was aware of what he was feeling and that he was unabashed about expressing it. That includes even negative feelings, the sense of weakness that he finds in himself. It is only because of his strong sense of self—paradoxically, his inalienable sense of self-esteem—that Paul could detect and admit to his weakness and infirmity.

What was mentioned, furthermore, in Chapter II about one's primordial commitment finds confirmation here. The relationship between Paul's commitment to the risen Lord and his commitment to others is the same as the relationship between one's primordial commitment and one's primary commitments. His commitment to people manifested, symbolized, and bodied forth his primordial commitment to the risen Lord. It would be a denial of the depth of change that took place in Paul not to have Christ Jesus present and operating at the most elemental, ontological roots of his existence (which is where we located one's primordial commitment).

The image of commitment to God that is entertained by far too many Christians is a caricature of Christian commitment because it seems to regard people as being worthy only of an afterthought, treated as leftovers after absolutizing the commitment to God far beyond reality. People were not expendable in order for Paul's commitment to God in Christ to be lived out, they were essential to it. To see this, one need only go back to the scene on the road to Damascus. Upon being knocked off his horse, Paul asks, "Who are you, Lord?" And he is told, "I am Jesus whom you are persecuting" (Acts 9:5). Jesus identifies himself so intimately with those who believe in him that belief in him cannot be disgorged from love of and commitment to his members. In Christ, Paul's capacity for friendship and love has attached itself to an infinite source of love; therefore, his capacity to give himself to others in love becomes extraordinary. One can read in his letters the enormous affection he feels toward specific individuals. His intense feelings for people can be looked on as proof of Jesus' promise that anyone who follows him will have family and friends a hundredfold.

The symbiosis that took place between Jesus and Paul

146

did not stop there. It extended out beyond Paul to an unending series of individuals. It was creative of communion, in other words. Each individual in this communion was caught up in the same symbiosis with Christ, but even more incredibly, with each other also. It was as if a whole group of people, though remaining individuals, had become one body. This is in fact what Paul eventually claims. To be in Christ is to be where a lot of other people are also, but this in turn deepens the degree of relationship one can expect of one another, since all have been made one reality, Christ's own body on earth. One can no longer stand apart, therefore, from others if in fact they are part of the same reality—as intimate to one another as a person is to his own body.

So much for Paul's love of individual Christians and Christian congregations. Can we say that Paul's commitment to God in Christ meant that he was also committed to the Church? Yes and no. Yes, insofar as the Church was Christ; yes, insofar as the Church was the body of Christ; yes, insofar as the Church was made up of Christians. Paul could not separate what God had joined together any more than the rest of us can, and what God had joined together, of course, was his Son and those who believed in his Son. But the answer to the question is no, insofar as the Church is also an intramundane reality and not the risen Lord. She was and is a pilgrim *simul justus et peccator;* she is both in need of and under the judgment of God.

Several other things might be said about Paul's commitment to the Church. He seems to have had the same *yes but* attitude toward the Church that Jesus had toward Israel. His tone is never ecclesiastical because his focus is never ecclesiocentric. Paul preached Christ to the churches. Why should the Church itself be what he preached? He would have been simply trading one form of zealotry for another, and zealotry he had enough of in his former days. He could, of course, have become anxious about the Church, and its needs could have begun to blur his vision. But, fortunately, he did not and he remained clear that the object of his commitment was the person of Christ, which, of course, included Christ's body; therefore, the object of his commitment could be said to be the whole Christ.

Paul could not be committed to Christ without being committed to the whole Christ, which includes his Church. But the way Paul ministered to the part of the body that he was attending to at any one moment was to get it in touch with its head. The way he loved the body that was Christ's own was to share with its members the Lord he loved and point them to their head and the source of his and their life. The more he pointed to the source of his own life, the more the communities to whom he witnessed came alive.

In brief, Paul shows how false it would be to try to spiritualize one's commitment to God in Christ by "including people out." Nor can one be said to be a Pauline Christian if one completely identifies Christ with the Church and, therefore, one's commitment to Christ with his commitment to the Church. This is too immanentist and doomed to make Christians parochial. On the other hand, one's commitment cannot be to God in Christ unless this is fleshed out with love of persons and communities.

In this chapter we have tried to see further into the mystery of commitment by reviewing some of the teachings of Jesus on the subject and by analyzing the commitment and the noncommitment of some New Testament figures. In the episode of the rich young man, we saw the intimate connection between redemption and the process of self-donation. The life of Mary gives further elucidations: the horizon shifts she was called on to accept in her relationship to God and her people; her successful resistance to the temptation of having the community spell out the contents of her commitment to God; the place of hope in a life of commitment.

Paul the apostle's life is also instructive in a number of ways. Although he was unswervingly committed to God throughout his life, when his optic about the personality of his God changed, the change in him was enormous. He began to show the characteristics of Christ in his own life. Because of the Spirit of Christ, Paul's indwelling of the person of Christ was intense and intimate. Paul's life as a Christian indicates that ideally an interpersonal commitment is not made, but it is yielded to in freedom and ratified in love. His life also shows the capacity for indwelling to be generative of communion rather than intimistic since there was no lessening of the intensity of Paul's commitment when he is laboring for the members of the whole Christ for whom he poured himself out like a libation. His brothers and sisters in Christ were one with the object of his commitment who was Christ crucified and risen.

Chapter VI
The Mystery of Fidelity

The problem with commitments is not so much making them, but keeping them. Judging by human behavior, at least, that must be the harder part. So our subject matter for this chapter moves from commitment to the question of fidelity. First we will inquire into how fidelity and commitment are related, then we will analyze the components of fidelity, and finally we will attempt to situate human fidelity in its religious and theological frame of reference.

In comparison to fidelity, commitment seems to be a brittle category. In comparison to fidelity, furthermore, commitment plays a relatively small part in a person's conscious life, it seems to me. On the other hand, I believe most of us expend a good deal of psychic energy trying to figure out what is entailed in order to be faithful to the reality we find ourselves in.

For those who have already made their commitments, commitments might no longer be a significant category. Commitment is like a door to be gone through, but once through it, fidelity or infidelity is the moral shape of the land entered. In other words, for one who has gone through the narrow gate, commitment is likely to be a nonproblem. Once inside the reality of a committed life, the problem of commitment passes over into a question of the manner of fidelity. It passes over into the interaction between the primordial direction of one's life and the ways one chooses to express this by word and action and relationship. In other words, I think there comes a time when commitment recedes as an operational aspect of one's life. We might call it a self-consuming artifact. It can re-emerge at any point, for a number of reasons, as a vital question. But the sooner one gets beyond it, so to speak, the greater the likelihood that one is living a committed life.

HUMAN FIDELITY

One aspect of fidelity has to do with the past. One does not live as if each moment of his life begins from zero. No, he comes from somewhere, and fidelity has to include adverting to what it is he has come from. The most formal determinations of our past, of course, are the doors we have come through to bring us where we are—our choices, in other words. But that's just part of it. One should not be faithful to the past as such, for that would be to seek the living among the dead. The past must be the source of our orientation to the future. At the same time, one's past cannot supply one with strength to continue into the future the commitments made in the past. The commitments one has made must authenticate themselves in the present. The fact that they were assumed in

SHOULD ANYONE SAY FOREVER?

the past is not sufficient reason in itself for their continuance. The faithful man never tries to live his life as if he
could disengage himself from his past, which means more
than taking his own history seriously. One could take one's
history seriously while regretting or tolerating the situation one is in. To be faithful one must not only take one's
past into account but also accept it in freedom anew and
choose it again as one's own, particularly as regards one's
commitments.

The ultimate criterion for fidelity cannot be continuity
with one's past or with the decisions one has made in the
past. To continue to maintain earlier choices is good only
if past decisions now produce, or give promise of produc-
ing, self-donation, indwelling and communion.

Fidelity has more to do with the present than with the
past. One of the consequences of commitment should be
to free one from a superficiality of presence to another or
others. Being faithful means, for starters, being fully
present in the relational situation in which one finds oneself. The faithful person lives facing into a "we are" horizon. What one is faithful to is the communion one is in or
is coming into or is hoping to come into. And at the center
of that communion is the indwelling one enjoys or hopes
to enjoy. Faithfulness has these realities as its purview.

What constitutes fidelity in one person's life would be
infidelity in another's. Only the individual will know ultimately what constitutes fidelity and infidelity for him.
People cannot be considered faithful if they are living in a
situation in which they are more absent than present to
one another. I am not referring to the amount of time
spent with the person or persons to whom one has committed himself. I am referring to the quality of the interac-

tion between them. Presence is indefinable, but it is unmistakable nonetheless. It creates indwelling and, in turn, communion, and strengthens them once they are there. Its opposite might involve physical presence, but it stops there. When nothing comes out from the person's heart, and nothing gets into it either, when the situation is affectively inert and barren, due to an intentional neglect of presence, this is infidelity.

There are instances in which the continuance of a seeming communion will be more destructive of the parties concerned than its discontinuance would be. In these cases the conscience of the individual(s) must be the ultimate court of appeal. For Christians, love of one another is the single commandment they are under. There are times when love will call for removing oneself from a commitment to another or others. One cannot be accused of unfaithfulness if one withdraws from the shell of a dead relationship. A nonexistent bond cannot be broken. Why it is nonexistent, of course, is another matter.

If it ever existed, the question of infidelity must be turned back to the causes of the actions (or inaction) that made the bond grow weaker and slighter until there was no bond at all. Communion is not a state of being that one enters and sleeps in. It is a dynamic of interrelationships that must be constantly nurtured. Fidelity involves being willing to generate the ingenuity needed to nurture the communion that is already present (or hoped for).

Some commitments are mistakes, of course. Since people make mistakes, they should not be treated like lepers the rest of their lives for their errors of judgment. But there are not as many mistaken commitments as there are claims that the commitment was a mistake. In fact, with-

SHOULD ANYONE SAY FOREVER?

drawal from a commitment is seldom called for. It is an
extreme reaction and rarely a solution to interpersonal
distress or communion gone stale. The fact that it has to
be used increasingly only proves that it is rarely a solution. What is much more often called for is conversion in
its literal sense, which means a simple turning of one's
heart back toward the other or others with whom one has
been in communion in whatever degree. Breaking one's
commitment is usually a way of avoiding the more likely
root of the problem, which is aversion from communion of
the hearts of one or more of the parties involved. Finding
problems with the commitment is a handy way of finding
a scapegoat and not facing up to the self-absorption or
dalliance or neglect of presence that caused the bond between the parties to be weakened in the first place.

A faithful person is not one whose heart stays in the
same place, since that is not the way hearts operate. They
are notoriously given to being vagrant and askew. The
faithful person is one who continues to center his or her
heart. Faithful persons do not cease to resituate themselves in the communion they are in. Fidelity is submis-
sion to the ongoing process of conversion. The only love
that does not need conversion is God's love for us. There
is no human love that is without the tendency to fall away
from presence; consequently, there is no interpersonal
commitment that can last without conversion in the sense
herein described.

Are there instances in which the commitment itself is
the source of the problem rather than the hearts of those
involved? There are such instances. There is justification
for withdrawal from those commitments in which no communion has taken place and none can be hoped for and

when, furthermore, the process of self-donation is being ignored or positively inhibited by the other party. Fidelity in these rare instances cannot be focused on a "we are," since it does not exist. It seems to me, then, to be a misunderstanding of the process of salvation itself to suggest that persons finding themselves in this kind of situation have to remain in it. Recall that previously in this study I pointed out how intimately linked salvation is with the process of self-donation. Where the latter is obstructed, one must have recourse to a more ultimate understanding of fidelity than the immediate interpersonal situation itself can provide to resolve the question of staying or leaving. But, as has also been said, I think this kind of situation is the exception.

How can I be sure that the problem is much more often in the hearts of the parties than in their commitment? Because of the nature of an interpersonal commitment. As we have seen, if a commitment really has been made, it creates a new reality. If one neglects to turn toward the one to whom one is supposedly committed, one will lapse back into habits acquired before—more precisely, into acting as if this new existential reality did not exist. "To posit myself in isolation from you is to be isolated in my actions from my own being,"[1] according to philosopher Robert O. Johann. Acting despite my commitments, in fact "committing myself to objects apart from you is to embark on a groundless course and to empty my life of meaning,"[2] he continues. Even when the significance of this kind of behavior is not seen or intended, its net effect

[1] Robert O. Johann, quoted from *Person and Community*, ed. by Robert Roth, S.J. (New York: Fordham University Press, 1975), p. 172.
[2] Loc. cit.

can be fatal to the commitment. All of which is to say that fidelity is being present to and acting in terms of the interpersonal reality one has entered into.

One often hears the expression, "You must be faithful to yourself." Fidelity to oneself is either a careless expression or a misguided notion. It is misguided if one thinks that the only criterion for fidelity is oneself. One has come from and is now part of a larger whole that has been created by choices and commitments. Not that the whole should define the part, but that the part should not act or think that the whole could self-destruct whenever the part wants to imagine itself autonomous.

I think a more careful use of language can clarify the point. "One must be true to oneself" is a more felicitous expression. It would be absurd to try to be faithful to others if one were not true to oneself. But that means that the precondition of fidelity is that one is true to oneself. Being true to oneself means something different throughout the course of one's life. We are always in process, which is to say we are never fully in possession of ourselves, or of a complete understanding of ourselves. Every moment of self-discovery creates a greater realization of the incomprehensibility of the self rather than satisfaction that one finally knows oneself. Fidelity to others presumes one is in touch with this self that is ever coming into being and into focus. Not to be in touch with this self as it is being born will certainly make one incapable of being faithful to others. A long term state of being out of touch with oneself inevitably leads to the creation of unreal liaisons posing as relationships and even false communions. Fidelity and commitment questions posed from that state are unanswerable.

GOD'S FIDELITY

One who believes in God cannot separate faithfulness in human relationships from God's own faithfulness. The links between these two expressions of fidelity are many and profound. Theologian Sam Keen has summarized Marcel's thought in this matter thusly: "Absolute fidelity to God will have no meaning in a world from which human fidelity has fled, nor is fidelity between persons possible unless there remains a veiled sense of the holy."[3] The way to be faithful to God is to be faithful to the promises we have made to him and each other. Fidelity, before it involves any particular action, requires an acceptance of the existential situation one has freely entered into. But to the believer the existential situation will always include and be open to the in-breaking reality of God.

Ultimately, I don't believe one can see into the mystery of fidelity by maintaining a purely secular perspective of interpersonal relations. The juridical, prudential approach to solving questions of fidelity in commitment is complex and finally dissatisfying. What is satisfying, on the other hand, is to plunge the interminable questions about what constitutes human fidelity into the theological realities of God's own life and his fidelity toward us.

Fidelity is a property of God's own life, not a quality that is natural to human beings. He is the faithful one. Interpersonal faithfulness consequently is intimately linked to one's ability to perceive God's faithfulness to us in general and oneself in particular. Human fidelity is a reflec-

[3] Sam Keen, *Gabriel Marcel* (Richmond: John Knox Press, 1967), p. 40.

tion of and a participation in God's faithfulness to us. The justification, in fact the necessity of a life of faith, should be obvious therefore if one would be faithful.

In the eyes of the Christian believer, the most immediate evidence of God's fidelity is, of course, Jesus. But before touching on the subject of Jesus' fidelity we will first describe the quality of God's faithfulness as it is revealed in the Hebrew Scriptures. This deserves treatment first if for no other reason than the fact that Jesus' own perception of God's fidelity came from, and was rooted in, these Scriptures.

Judging from the number of times it is mentioned and described in the Old Testament, Yahweh must have thought it was of primary importance for Israel to know his quality of faithfulness. The Hebrew word for it is *hesed*, which cannot be translated neatly by any one English word, since it means to convey the dual motions of steadfastness and tenderness or love and fidelity.

The perception of God's fidelity, like any perception of divine reality, has to be seen through its analogy with material things. It is obvious in a number of places in Scripture that Israel was being led to see the evidence of Yahweh's fidelity in nature. Signs of this were omnipresent to the scriptural writers. Israel traced every instance of constancy she was aware of in the order of nature to Yahweh and to Yahweh's creative word. "By the word of Yahweh the heavens were made, their whole array by the breath of his mouth" (Ps. 33:6). Not only are the Israelites invited to see his power in the cosmic order in contrast to their powerlessness, and his creativity in contrast to their contingency, but they are encouraged to see his faithfulness in creation. Their response to seeing his faithfulness, his hesed, manifested in nature, was worship and praise of him. The sun, the moon, and the stars, the waters and all that were in them, the beasts of the fields, the birds of the air, and every manner of living things were there and are still there witnessing to his fidelity and to the fact that his word once spoken has never been rescinded. The sight of the birds of the air being fed and the lilies of the fields being clothed could be a constant reminder to a believing Israelite that God does not withdraw the slightest detail of the word that he speaks.

The Hebrew Scriptures would have the Israelites connect the faithfulness of Yahweh as it was seen in the beauty and order and harmony and continuing fecundity of creation with Yahweh's choice of Israel and his faithfulness to her as a people. For example: "Yahweh says this, 'if you could break my covenant with the day and my covenant with the night so that day and night do not come in their due time, then my covenant with David my servant might also be broken'" (Jer. 33:19–20). Or, another example: "Yahweh who provides the sun for light by day, the moon and stars for light by night, who stirs the sea, making its waves roar, he whose name is Yahweh Sabaoth, says this: 'were this established order ever to pass away from my presence—it is Yahweh who speaks—only then would the race of Israel also cease to be a nation in my presence forever,'" (Jer. 31:35–36). Finally, "David's dynasty shall last forever, I see his throne like the sun, enduring forever like the moon, that faithful witness in the sky" (Ps. 89:36–37).

Creation, however, was not as persuasive in Israel's eyes of Yahweh's faithfulness as the events by which he fulfilled every promise he had ever made to her. Through the exodus events, the promise to Abraham began to be fulfilled. Through the conquests of Canaan, the promise that this people would possess their own land began to be realized. In the forty-year period between the exodus event and their entrance into the land of Canaan, he continually disciplined his people and formed them so that above all else they could see that he was faithful. His fidelity to Israel was not sporadic. In the Patriarchs and Prophets, the Judges and the Kings, he showed himself as one who keeps his word. By his sovereign acts of deliverance of Israel from her enemies his fidelity begins to write itself into the character of his people.

His fidelity takes on a form. Yahweh commits himself to his people, and the form that his commitment takes is that of a covenant. He enters into a covenant with Israel. By reason of the covenant Yahweh creates, as it were, a communion which specifies, both for himself and for his people Israel, the entire future. By reason of this particularization he realigns his relationship to all other peoples. Henceforth and forever all the nations of the earth will be blessed through his chosen nation.

But Israel, stiff-necked Israel, was unimpressed. In the teeth of their unresponsiveness Yahweh continues to enflesh his love and choice of Israel. Notwithstanding the long periods in which she wonders whether or not she wants the covenant relationship that he extends to her, his fidelity endures. The prophet Hosea employs a most powerful image to express the degree of the communion that Yahweh desires to enter into with Israel when he employs the image of marriage. Hosea was appalled at the disparity between the marriage partners, Israel and Yahweh, but that did not keep him from communicating the vision of intimacy that opened up to him.

God projects a time within the covenant relationship when the communion between himself and his people will be total. The time will come when he will put his own Spirit within them; a union so complete that they will be animated by his own Spirit. The communion between him and his people then will be as everlasting as God's own life. "I will make an everlasting covenant with them" (Jer. 32:40). The way that this state of affairs will come about: "I shall put my Spirit in you, and you will live, and I shall resettle you on your own soil" (Ezek. 37:14).

In varying degrees Yahweh manifested himself to Israel, but the height of his love was manifested by reason of, and through his fidelity to, his covenant. By reason of the covenant Israel was able to perceive the inner characteristic of God's own life, his hesed. Because of this quality he made the covenant, and at the same time, by his keeping the covenant, this quality became manifest to believing Israel.

Israel's response to Yahweh's hesed was meant to create a human reflection in her of that divine quality. But Israel was never consistent in her response to Yahweh's steadfast love of her. Faithful she was not. For long stretches of her history she tried to take her destiny into her own hands as if she had come into existence like any other nation. She sought to create a communion of her own making by currying the favor of other gods and imitating the practices of other nations. She hired herself out to other lovers like a whore, seeking from others what Yahweh pledged he alone could provide her with. She sought security within herself, and tried regarding herself as self-sufficient and capable of clothing herself with prosperity. But she was not a nation like other nations. Therefore, she did not succeed in clothing herself with power or with the things of the earth, since she existed solely because of Yahweh's choice of her and his fidelity to the covenantal relationship he had entered into with her.

Her lack of response did not result in his withdrawal of the communion he had established. He taught her his fidelity by allowing her to feel the effects of her turning away from his steadfast love. What felt like Yahweh's wrath to them and what they called his wrath was actually Yahweh's way of allowing Israel to feel in her bones the divorce which her neglect of the covenant had effectively produced in her. If he were not faithful, she would not have had an awareness of her own sinfulness and desperation. But again and again he allows her to feel her nakedness before her enemies, whom she tried to compete with and whose gods she tried to be clothed by. Humiliated, she turns back to him. Hers in a history of oscillation between aversion and conversion.

Hosea recounts this experience starkly: "I will make a wilderness of her, turn her into an arid land and leave her to die of thirst . . . when the time comes I mean to withdraw my corn and my wine . . . my wool, my flax which were intended to cover her nakedness; so will I display her shame before her lover's eyes and no one shall rescue her from my power . . . then she will say I will go back to my husband, I was happier then than I am today" (Hos. 2:3–16). If his love of Israel did not include the quality of faithfulness, then the communion between the two of them would have dissolved by Israel's turning away. But besides being loving he was also faithful, which meant that he remained true to the order that was created by his word and his covenant. Consequently, for him to be faithful included his letting Israel feel the disorder which she had caused. She learned anew and more deeply of his faithfulness because of the grief she came to through her unfaithfulness.

Yahweh persisted: "I am going to lure and lead her out into the wilderness and speak to her . . . then she will respond to me as she did when she was young" (Hos. 2:14–15). A chastened Israel could proclaim with the Psalmist: "I will celebrate your love forever, Yahweh, age after age my words shall proclaim your faithfulness; for I claim that love is built to last forever and your faithfulness founded firmly in the heavens" (Ps. 89:1–2).

Yahweh's fidelity was evident in the fact that he was ever turned toward Israel: "His face shone upon her and she was glad." The fidelity he looked for in return was for Israel to be turned toward him. But her heart was seldom centered in depth or at length in her Lord. She was exhorted again and again to turn back to him—to submit to the process of conversion, in other words. It was not the practices of the law that he sought, it was her heart. It was not even her sinlessness and innocence that he sought, but the admission of her powerlessness and nakedness when she went beyond the pale which his love had created. Notwithstanding repeatedly learning this lesson by feeling in her bones the result of trying to make it turned away from Yahweh, Israel was never faithful very long nor God-reliant very deeply. Her response was always wanting, her heart divided.

She needed a Messiah to teach her to see and be responsive to Yahweh's hesed. Jesus was the perfect human response to Yahweh's hesed. "The son of God, the Christ Jesus that we proclaim among you . . . was never Yes and No: with him it was always Yes, and however many the promises God made, the Yes to them all is in Him. That is why it is through Him that we answer Amen to the praise of God" (II Cor. 1:19–20). Jesus' response to his Father brings into human focus the quality of faithfulness that Yahweh sought from his people. That is one aspect of it. The other is that Jesus is God's yes to his own promises. With the sending of his Son we can see that God keeps his promises. Jesus is the enfleshment of Yahweh's hesed. This inner characteristic of God's own life becomes visible in the eternal Son made man. Since he combines these two kinds of fidelity—God's to his chosen people and theirs to God—Jesus deserves again to be described as mediator between God and humankind. Jesus is the perfect manifestation of God's faithfulness, and being in union with him is our way of having our lives reflect the hesed of God.

Jesus grounds the previously established covenant between God and Israel in the reality of his own life. On the night before he died he fully subsumed into his person the commitment that Yahweh had made to Israel. "This cup is the new covenant in my blood, the blood which will be poured out for you" (Luke 22:20). Jesus is the new form of God's commitment to the new Israel, and the Eucharist is the symbol of this commitment. Henceforth, God's steadfast kindness toward us will be shown in and through his Son and first and foremost by this symbol. Each Eucharist is a renewal and a reaffirmation on God's part of the bond he has created between us and himself in his Son. It is God in Christ's way of again and again embedding his "yes" to us in our lives. Through the Eucharist we can say yes to one another in the communions that exist among us believers. Finally, each Eucharist is a time to strengthen and celebrate anew the ultimate dimensions of whatever communion we are in, which is the eternal communion of Father, Son, and Spirit.

This chapter has complemented our analysis of commitment with the theme of fidelity. It suggests that the relationship between the two is that of a gate to the reality one enters by passing through it. If commitment is the gate, then fidelity is the reality one faces having arrived. An ongoing conversion of heart was seen as necessary to be true to the reality one has come to through commitment.

But fidelity to one another was seen as having a greater intelligibility if it were viewed as a reflection of the faithfulness of God toward humankind. The Christian will see this fidelity primarily in Jesus whose coming showed God's faithfulness to his promises and whose living among us revealed the ultimate example of the life of faithfulness. The Eucharist was then viewed in terms of fidelity.

Being faithful to God and one another is made easier if one is in Christ since he is the perfect "yes" to the Father. The mystery of commitment and fidelity reaches the heights of intelligibility in the person of Jesus without at the same time ceasing to be mystery.

> Jesus spoke to them again:
> I tell you most solemnly,
> I am the gate of the sheepfold.
> (John 10:7)

Our study began with the image, except that now the gate can be more fully identified. It is Christ himself. John's Gospel does not dwell on this somewhat awkward image but goes on to describe Jesus as a shepherd to those who are determined to live in him.

Anyone who enters through me will be safe:
he will go freely in and out
and be sure of finding pasture.
(John 10:8)

I believe that the shepherd's favorite way of enabling his sheep to be faithful to him and one another is to put his own Spirit within them. This Gift makes human fidelity one in stature and dignity with God's fidelity to us. It provides those who are his with a spring within themselves, as it were, whose power can propel them in a straight line all the way to eternal life.

Q39